VALUE FOR MONEY AUDITING
IN THE PUBLIC SECTOR

Research Studies in Accounting   Series Editor: B. V. Carsberg

VALUE FOR MONEY
AUDITING IN
THE PUBLIC SECTOR

John J. Glynn

Department of Economics, Exeter University

Prentice/Hall   PHI   International

Englewood Cliffs, NJ   London   New Delhi   Rio de Janeiro
Singapore   Sydney   Tokyo   Toronto   Wellington

In association with

The Institute of Chartered Accountants in England and Wales

British Library Cataloguing in Publication Data
Glynn, John J.
  Value for money auditing in the public sector.
  —(ICAEW accounting research series)
  1. Finance, Public—Great Britain—
  Accounting   2. Management audit
  I. Title   II. Institute of Chartered
  Accountants in England and Wales   III. Series
  657'.45   HJ9925.G6

This book consists of a research study undertaken on behalf of The Institute of Chartered Accountants in England and Wales. In publishing this book the Institute considers that it is a worthwhile contribution to discussion but neither Institute nor the Research Board necessarily shares the views expressed, which are those of the author alone.

No responsibility for loss occasioned to any person acting or refraining from action as a result of any material in this publication can be accepted by the author or publisher.

ISBN 0-13-940347 7

Prentice-Hall International Inc., London
Prentice-Hall of Australia Pty. Ltd., Sydney
Prentice-Hall Canada, Inc., Toronto
Prentice-Hall of India Private Ltd., New Delhi
Prentice-Hall of Japan, Inc., Tokyo
Prentice-Hall of Southeast Asia Pte, Ltd., Singapore
Prentice-Hall Inc., Englewood Cliffs, New Jersey
Prentice-Hall do Brasil Ltda., Rio de Janeiro
Whitehall Books Ltd., Wellington, New Zealand

10 9 8 7 6 5 4 3 2 1

Printed in the United Kingdom by A. Wheaton and Company Ltd., Exeter

To John and Kathleen Glynn, my parents

Contents

6 AUDIT: ONE ASPECT OF PUBLIC FINANCIAL CONTROL

Foreword

When the Institute of Chartered Accountants set up its Research Board and appointed me as its Director of Research, we carried out a consultative process in order to identify the areas of research which should be given priority in the Board's programme of work. The subject of value for money auditing was accorded a high degree of priority in the programme.

John Glynn's report makes a significant contribution to our understanding of the principles and practice underlying the subject. It is perhaps indicative of the newness of the discipline that considerable controversy surrounds the question of what comprises, or ought to comprise, value for money auditing. If John Glynn's report sheds light on that issue, and I believe it does, that alone is a useful contribution. Whether value for money is characterised in simple terms such as "absence of waste" or in the more analytical framework of "economy, efficiency and effectiveness", its measurement must be an important goal. Value for money auditing has emerged naturally in the public sector of the economy where the absence of relatively firm measures of profitability creates particular difficulty in judging performance. However, applications of the measurement process can make important contributions to efficiency in the private sector as well as the public.

One of the main objectives of the Institute's research programme is to stimulate thinking and ultimately contribute to the improvement of practic in areas that are of importance to its members. *Value for Money Auditing* is central to that objective. Its subject brings new challenges to the world of practice, requiring radical changes in the outlook of accountants, but it also brings new opportunities. Readers will not agree with all John Glynn's views, but I am confident that they will benefit from his sharing of experiences in this important topic.

Bryan Carsberg
Director of Research

Acknowledgements

In submitting this project I should like briefly to mention some of those who have assisted me:

— to Professor R. H. Parker, Exeter University, for his useful comments on writing style and presentation;

— to Graham Stacy and Tom Walls at Price Waterhouse and Professor Alan Barton, Australian National University, Canberra, for the provision of research facilities;

— to Doug Hill, Deputy-Auditor General, Commonwealth of Australia; Professor John Perrin, Warwick University and David Shand, Senior Director, Auditor General's Office for the State of Victoria for comments on earlier drafts of this monograph;

— to Margaret Pollock, Australian National University, Canberra, for administrative assistance, Alison Henderson for meticulous proof reading and Helen Goody for typing the final drafts of this monograph.

John J. Glynn

Abbreviations

APC	Auditing Practices Committee
C&AG	Comptroller and Auditor General
CCAB	Consultative Committee of Accounting Bodies
CICA	Canadian Institute of Chartered Accountants
CIPFA	Chartered Institute of Public Finance and Accountancy
DOE	Department of the Environment
E&AD	Exchequer and Audit Department
FASB	Financial Accounting Standards Board
FSBR	Financial Statement and Budget Report
GAO	General Accounting Office (US)
GLC	Greater London Council
NAB	National Audit Bureau (Sweden)
PAC	Public Accounts Committee
POUNC	Post Office Users National Council
PPBS	Planning Programming Budgeting Systems
SCNI	Select Committees on Nationalised Industries
ZBB	Zero Base Budgeting

1

The Need For Value For Money Audits

Value for Money (VFM) audits have developed in recent years as a way of expanding the more traditional role of the auditor away from a straightforward examination of the fairness of the financial statements of an organization.

Particularly in Canada, Sweden and the United States, these expanded forms of audit have been applied to many non-profit organizations; though these are mainly in the areas of central and local governments and their agencies. Their current introduction into the British public sector represents the only constructive development in the, as yet, unresolved debate on the general reform of public accountability and audit.

In this first chapter we endeavour to do two things in order to set in context the discussion of the succeeding chapters. These are, firstly, to provide some background by providing information on the size of the public sector and by citing

some recent examples that indicate a growing awareness of

the need for greater accountability within the public sector.

Secondly, arguments are presented in favour of the

introduction of VFM audits.

Background To The Problem

One of the great architects of the Canadian Public Service,

Arnold Heeney, wrote in his memoirs (p. 14):

"In a complex society which makes ever-increasing demands on
government, a large and complicated public service is
inevitable. Great size and complexity carry with them
terrible dangers, chiefly of course, the dangers commonly
associated with the word 'bureaucracy'."

How large then is our public sector?   In the Government

White Paper on Public Expenditure (Cmnd 8789-I) the planned

expenditure of 1983-84 is £119.6 billion which represents an

expected 44% of gross domestic product (GDP).   (This is not

exceptionally high among developed European nations.)

This expenditure can be subdivided under three main headings:

		£ million	%
(i)	Central Government	88,608	74
(ii)	Nationalized Industries	2,625	2
(iii)	Local Authorities	28,234	24
		119,467	100

Under the heading Central Government expenditure, rather less
than half the figure is for goods and services, mainly for
defence and the national health service. Slightly over
one-third is for social security benefits, with just under
10% allocated for civil service pay and associated costs.
The remainder represents transfer payments, such as housing
subsidies, industrial support and lending to the nationalized
industries (£1,113 million).

In recent years public expenditure in Britain has jumped
dramatically, often increasing, in money terms, by more than
10% per annum. For the financial year 1980–81 the expenditure,
at £92.6 billion, was an increase on the previous year of
more than 20%. This was a period of high inflation and the
present Conservative Government came to power with a manifesto
which stated that it would improve efficiency and limit
waste in the public sector. To do this they have attempted
to enforce a strict financial climate, including the use of

cash limits and cash planning, to motivate public servants

towards greater economy and efficiency. Currently (1983/84)

40% of public expenditure is directly cash-limited. This

includes the external financing limits imposed on nationalized

industries. Another 40% consists of 'demand-determined'

services where, once policy and rates of payment have been

determined, expenditure in the short-term depends on the

number of qualifying applicants; for example, social security

benefits. The remaining 20% represents local authority

current expenditure; the rate support grant, the government's

main contribution to financing such expenditure.

The White Paper only envisages an increase in public

expenditure of approximately 5% per annum for the next few

years.

In addition to cash limits, other actions, including new

legislation, have also been introduced to improve value for

money in public spending. Section 15 of the Local Government

Finance Act 1982 lays down the general duties of a local

government auditor. These are to satisfy himself that

accounts are properly prepared and that local authorities

have made proper arrangements for securing economy,

efficiency and effectiveness in the use of its resources;

and to report on matters of public interest which come to

his attention.

The wording of this section is very wide and therefore

provides the auditor with a great deal of discretion and

flexibility in the performance of his duties. For example,

he is to satisfy himself "by examination of the accounts and

otherwise" about the authorities' practices, procedures and

accounts. The statutory requirement to look at procedures

for securing "effectiveness" is new. Further, the Act

provides no guidance as to what constitutes "the public

interest".

It could be claimed that local government had already

embarked upon policies of value for money as witnessed by

the following three pronouncements:

(a) The DOE's 'Code of Practice for External Audit' (1973)
     states: "he (the auditor) must be concerned not only
     with the form and regularity of the accounts but also
     with issues of substance arising therefrom, such as the
     possibility of loss due to waste, extravagance,
     inefficient financial administration, poor value for
     money, mistake or other cause".

(b) CIPFA's statement, 'Role and Objectives of Internal
     Audit in the Public Sector' (1979) states: "it is the
     responsibility of internal audit to review, appraise
     and report on .... the extent to which organization's
     assets and interest are accounted for and safe-guarded
     from losses of all kinds arising from fraud and other
     offences; waste, extravagance and inefficient
     administration; poor value for money or other cause".

VMA-B

(c)   CIPFA's statement, 'Draft Standards for the External
      Audit of Local Authorities' (1981) states:
      "The auditor should seek to identify those activities
      of the authority which have either suffered a loss or
      are exposed to the risk of loss due to lack of adequate
      procedures for securing economy, efficiency and
      effectiveness in the use of resources".

Whilst some local authorities have taken a lead by

appointing specialist staff for VFM exercises or sought aid

from external auditors and consultants, many other

authorities have not. All authorities will now need to do so

with the passing of this Act. Section 11 provides for the

appointment of an Audit Commission consisting of not less

than thirteen and not more than seventeen members appointed

by the Secretary of State for the Environment. The first

appointments of members have been made and the Audit Commission

has been functioning since 1 April 1983. All appointments

as auditor(s) to local authorities will be made by the

Commission. Previously, under the Local Government Act

1972, local authorities could appoint their own auditors,

who could either be the District Auditor or a firm approved

by the Secretary of State.

All the signs are that the Commission will expect auditors

to produce 'hard-hitting' factual reports that will vary in

both style and content from those previously produced.

Further discussion of the nature of such reports is to be

found in Chapter 4. Appendix A provides a summary of

Part III of the Local Government Finance Act 1982; that is, those provisions which relate to the audit of local authorities and other public bodies.

In another area of the public sector, the National Health Service, there have recently been awards of contracts to private sector auditing firms. These trial contracts for the audit of District Health Authorities require firms to spend about 40% of their time on VFM work. Eight pilot contracts were awarded in the autumn of 1981 and a further six contracts were awarded in the spring of 1983.

The Exchequer and Audit Department carry out some VFM work either as part of their regulatory work or sometimes as a separate, 'follow-up' exercise. David Dewar, a Deputy Secretary in the Exchequer and Audit Department, has quoted two examples of the work recently carried out by this department:

"One often finds on examining a grant scheme or other programme that expediture is in accordance with regulations and conditions of grant; but it is nevertheless not what was intended when the scheme was set up, or appears wasteful or extravagant. For example, grants under EEC provisions may properly be paid to farmers who meet conditions laid down for changing from milk to beef production, but VFM considerations arise if those farmers would have made the change anyway or had already done so. Again, hundreds of millions of pounds of Regional Development Grant were quite properly paid to firms building oil terminals in Orkney and Shetland; but we reported to the Public Accounts Committee,

amongst other things, that even without any grants, the
terminals would have been sited there for economic and
geological reasons."[1]

By contrast, Colville and Tomkins point to some contradictory

statements by the Comptroller and Auditor General on the

role of VFM auditing. They state (p.18):

"it appears that C & AG is, to some extent a reluctant
effectiveness auditor and, in pleading reluctance, he avoids
the necessity of having a clear statement of objectives of
how effectiveness audit should be conducted..."

These recent developments, together with other changes in

the public sector, provide a means whereby the public can

gain increased assurance that public servants managing their

resources are being held accountable for performance and

results.

Britain has never undertaken a comprehensive review of its

overall financial administration in the public sector,[2]

although it is true that, as will be discussed in Chapter 6,

there has been much recent, and fraught, debate on the role

of the Comptroller and Auditor General. Most recently The

National Audit Act received the Royal assent on 13 May 1983.

It is a brief document. Section 1 (3) states that:

"Subject to any duty imposed on him by statute, the
Comptroller and Auditor General shall have complete discretion
in the discharge of his functions, in particular, in
determining whether to carry out any examination under

Part III of this Act and as to the manner in which such
examination is carried out; but in determining whether to
carry out such examination he shall take into account any
proposals made by the Committee of Public Accounts."

Part II of this Act is titled 'Economy, Efficiency and

Effectiveness Examinations' and outlines those departments

and authorities that may be subject to review. However,

this most recent piece of legislation still leaves many

questions unanswered.

Canada, on the other hand, has undertaken such a review. A

Royal Commission on 'Financial Management and Accountability'

presented its final report in March 1979. It was the

Commission's view (p.21) that:

"the serious malaise pervading the management of Government
stems fundamentally from a grave weakening, and in some
cases an almost total breakdown, in the chain of
accountability, first within Government, and second in the
accountability of Government to Parliament and ultimately to
the Canadian people."

This Commission was hastily convened following comments made

by the Auditor General in his report for the fiscal year

ended 31 March 1976. In that report (p.9) the Auditor

General had declared:

"I am deeply concerned that Parliament – and indeed the
Government – has lost, or is close to losing, effective
control of the public purse ..... Based on the study of the
systems of departments, agencies and Crown Corporations

audited by the Auditor General, financial management and
control in the Government of Canada is grossly inadequate.
Furthermore, it is likely to remain so until the Government
takes strong, appropriate measures to rectify this critically
serious situation."

These were strong words. The emphasis in that statement

(shown underlined) was contained in the original report at

the behest of the Auditor General. Spending by all

governments in Canada exceeded 40% of GDP when the Commission

was set up.

One wonders what the reaction of the British Parliament and

public would be if our Comptroller and Auditor General ever

produced such a damning statement on the state of our

bureaucratic government administrative machine. There are,

though, increasing signs of disquiet.

In Parliament individual members have voiced their concern

on this question and called for corrective legislative action.

Mr Edward du Cann, a former chairman of the Public Accounts

Committee, told the House of Commons[3] that in his opinion

the Exchequer and Audit Department Act of 1866 was obsolete;

it restricted the state audit body in various ways and limited

the field it could cover. For this reason Parliament was

without access to inside information about the vast public

expenditure incurred indirectly through local authorities,

nationalized industries and subsidised bodies of all kinds.

He called for an immediate enquiry into the whole subject of

public accountability, given that "the control of public

expenditure is near the top of the charts recording the

public interest".

In addition to individual members of Parliament, the all-party

Public Accounts Committee does, from time to time, make

useful contributions to the debate on public accountability.

As will be clear by now, most of the recent changes in the

field of auditing are to be found in Local Government.

Other areas within the public sector are equally in need of

reform. Parliamentary control over nationalized industries

rests with various select committees whose work centres

around the sponsoring departments. These are shown in

Table 1.

Committees can call for both oral and written evidence when

investigating the managing of a particular industry. In

addition, there is the important Treasury Committee which

can investigate any financial matter concerning the links

between public finance and the nationalized industries.

The problem with these committees is that their resources

TABLE 1   SELECT COMMITTEE REVIEWS OF NATIONALIZED INDUSTRIES

Sponsoring Department	Industry
Energy	British Gas, Electricity, British National Oil Company, National Coal Board
Industry	British Steel, Post Office, British Shipbuilders, National Bus, British Rail, British Transport, Docks, National Freight
Trade	British Airways, British Airports Authority
Environment	British Waterways

are limited and their approach, despite no doubt good intent,

is often ad hoc.

Another ad hoc approach to public accountability is provided

by the Monopolies and Mergers Commission (MMC) whose reports

often provide an extensive insight into the financial and

administrative problems of particular nationalized industries.

Their investigatory powers are provided by Section 11 of the

Competition Act 1980, whereby the Secretary of State for

Trade can direct the MMC to investigate efficiency, costs,

the level and quality of service provided and possible misuse

of monopoly power within nationalized industries. Section

12 of this Act states that the Secretary of State may order

an industry to draw up a remedial plan if, and only to the

extent that, an industry is found to be pursuing a course of

action which is "against the public interest". The problem

is that several of the items that are cited in these reports

cannot individually be deemed serious enough to warrant the

specific direction of the Secretary of State and so often

are not capable of being amended. Typically these are items

which could well come within a VFM audit report and would

therefore be subject to future enquiry and follow up.

Nationalized industry chairmen, at present, seem to be quite

content that their external, private sector, auditors continue with financial audit procedures that, as far as possible,

mirror those found in the private sector. By contrast their

individual consumer councils very often voice complaints

that would suggest that they were not so entirely happy.

For example, Report No 24 of the Post Office Users Council

(POUNC) states:

"Government sets financial targets for the nationalized
industries. But customers at present have difficulty in
knowing whether they are getting value for money. It is
necessary to relate financial requirements, operational
performance and quality of service. The Post Office and its
unions have entered into agreements which are designed to
improve productivity. Customers are entitled to know how
they will benefit. We propose that the Post Office should
establish a procedure with POUNC to evaluate the performance
of the postal service against agreed yardsticks. Government
should agree the procedure and the yardsticks to be adopted.
A regular and open procedure to 'audit' the Post Office's
performance would, in our view, do more to promote the
interests of customers than the present arrangements."

Despite limitations, some improvements, founded on recent

legislation, are to be found within the local authorities

and nationalized industries but few moves (modest developments

in the National Health Service excepted) are, as yet, in

hand for the improved public accountability of Central

Government expenditure which, as shown earlier, accounts for

74% of the total.

Anthony (1971) when considering the general question of

whether US non-profit organizations could be well managed,

thought that he could only answer with a qualified "yes".

In his discussion he listed six reasons for the "deplorable

state of affairs" that exists in many organizations in the

United States.

These were (1) an absence of a profit measure, (2) the

absence of competition, (3) politics, (4) weak governing

boards, (5) tradition, and (6) low management salaries. His

qualified reply was subject to the resolution, as far as is

practicable, of these issues. In Britain, this check list

would appear equally appropriate when judging the performance

of many public sector bodies.

There are indeed many problems associated with measuring the

output of such organisations as the notion of providing a

service is often difficult to state in tangible/measurable

terms. As Anthony states (p. 9):

"The difficulty of defining objectives, of deciding on the
resources required to reach objectives, and of measuring the
efficiency and effectiveness with which the organisation's
performance meets objectives is, I believe, the most serious
management problem in a non-profit organisation. It is an
inherent problem; that is, there is no foreseeable way of
developing a control structure in a non-profit organisation
that is as good as a structure that can be built around the
profit measure."

In Chapters 2 and 3 we shall consider possible methods of

defining objectives and suitable output measures against

which performance can be gauged.

It is true that very often there is an absence of competition

within non-profit organizations. However, it may be possible

to promote the use of comparative statistics (see Chapter 2).

Many service centres within local authorities have now become

'direct labour organizations'. Under this scheme, a service

department, for example the buildings and maintenance

department, will have to tender a price in competition with

external agencies. If successful the contract will have to

be undertaken within the tender price, losses being borne by

that department.

Anthony points to a conflict that all politicians face; that

is, the trade-off between constituency interests and national

priorities. These may often not be the same and, presumably,

if he/she wishes future re-election his opinions may, not

unnaturally, be biased. Politicians are inevitable and

necessary in a democracy but individual and party political

influence need to be monitored by committees and working

parties whose deliberations help provide a more impartial

contribution to parliamentary debate.

External supervisory bodies very often lack real power, but

here again improvements can be made to prevent such bodies

from simply rubberstamping policies presented by top

management. For example, the National Health Service

re-organization in 1982 provided for the appointment of a
salaried part-time Chairman for each District Health
Authority.

By tradition, Anthony means the general lack of management
expertise whereby technically qualified people are often
designated as departmental heads. To continue with the
Health Service analogy, often a medical specialist is in
charge of a particular department because he or she is
technically very competent. However, he or she may not be
able to co-ordinate the activities of fellow clinicians and
support staff in attaining the best use of resources available.
The primary qualification for a departmental manager is to
be a good administrator: Bad administration is often a reason
why new management techniques are not adopted. To correct
this, technical specialists need to understand basic management
techniques which should be a pre-requisite for certain career
paths. Salary scales should also be increased to encourage
an interest in administrative positions.

Readers wishing to obtain a wider background to more general
public sector issues should consult the bibliography, in
particular the references to: Heald, D.; Henley, D.; Hepworth,
N.P.; Perrin, J.; Redwood, J. and Hatch, J; and Sherer, M.
and Kent, D.

In Favour Of Value For Money Auditing

Accountability in the public sector occurs when both
politicians and the public at large are assured that public
funds are being spent efficiently, economically and on
programmes that are effective. VFM auditing assists this
process by reporting upon management's performance at both
central and devolved Government levels.

Value for money can be thought of as consisting of three
elements: ECONOMY, EFFICIENCY AND EFFECTIVENESS. The first
two of these elements are fairly uncontroversial but the
third element, effectiveness, is both hard to define and
difficult to measure. (Chapters 2 and 3 discuss each element
at length.)

Control over the effectiveness of Government activities
involves the fulfilment of political goals by effective
administration. Figure 1 provides a brief illustration of
this process. The diagram depicts the development of
political goals into parliamentary legislation or ministerial
direction in order to provide the plans from which devolved
departments (or agencies) proceed to day-to-day implementation.
The diagram also shows the various stages at which the three
elements of value for money enter the cycle. The use of the

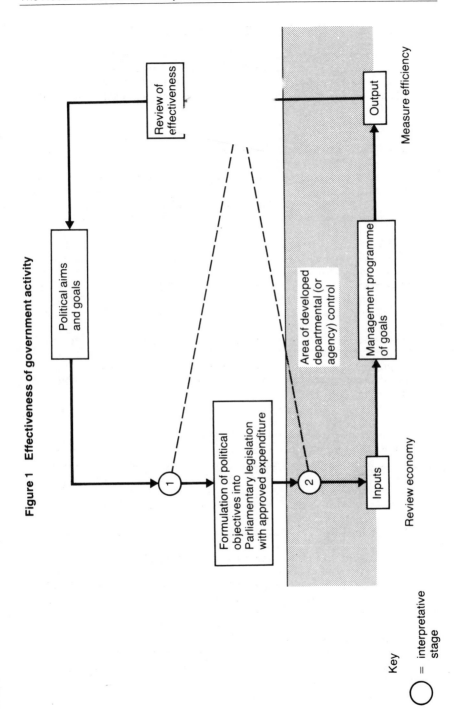

Figure 1 Effectiveness of government activity

Review of effectiveness

Political aims and goals

Formulation of political objectives into Parliamentary legislation with approved expenditure

1

2

Area of developed departmental (or agency) control

Inputs

Management programme of goals

Output

Measure efficiency

Review economy

Key

○ = interpretative stage

word <u>devolved</u> is intentional since, whilst formalized

channels of communication exist for the conveyance of policy,

service implementation is often determined at local level.

Until recently, there would normally have been two

interpretative stages. Whilst the first is mainly the result

of political debate and inevitable compromise, the second

stage arises as a result of translating diffuse policy

decisions into concrete plans for action. The third stage,

which leads to a review of effectiveness, is a new stage

that is becoming increasingly demanded.

VFM auditing provides regular and systematic feedback to

those responsible for the initial formulation of objectives.

This review operation is one that is well suited to the

diagnostic and interpretative skills of the auditor,

particularly since there are financial implications, which

always have a bearing on overall financial strategy, in all

govenment activities.

How is VFM auditing different from traditional auditing or

management consultancy? A conventional audit of financial

statements is designed to provide independent, objective

opinion that financial information prepared by management

has been presented fairly. As part of the process, the

auditor may include an examination of accounting and
information systems and may make recommendations to
management to improve these systems. Generally, audit
reports are predictable and short because the auditor is
guided by generally accepted accounting and audit principles
and standards.

Management consulting assignments generally require solutions
to perceived problems and experience at implementing solutions.
They may frequently involve advice on specialized management
decisions or implementing specialized management systems.
The range of situations, solutions and systems is very diverse.
There is no predictable form of reporting, and there are no
'generally accepted' standards for decision-making or systems
to guide the consultant.

VFM auditing is a blend of both conventional auditing and
management consulting. It benefits from the independence,
objectivity, and reporting skills of auditors, complemented
by the specialised analytical systems and implementation
skills that may be available from management consultants.
The report should be attention directing rather than
providing detailed solutions.

The wider adoption of VFM auditing will put new demands on

the auditor. In the words of the Canadian Adams Report

(p.39):

"The role of auditors is constantly evolving in response to
changing public needs and expectations. Although the primary
function of auditors is to add credibility to financial
information, recent developments seem to indicate a growing
trend towards viewing them in a broader context as agents of
social control, as third-party intermediaries in an
accountability relationship between the management of an
enterprise and the users of its information."

The Office of the Auditor General of Canada has developed an

acronym FRAME which identifies and explains the components

of a VFM audit (or in their terms 'Comprehensive Audit'):

F   Financial Controls - an evaluation of the controls over
    revenues, expenditures, assets and liaibilities, including
    the organization of the financial function and its place
    in the general management structure; the qualifications
    and suitability of financial personnel to the needs of
    the organization; the appropriateness of the accounting
    systems and procedures, and the appropriateness and
    adequacy of budgeting and financial reporting systems.

R   Reporting to Parliament - an evaluation of the nature,
    content, adequacy, reliability and timeliness of financial
    and related nonfinancial information presented in reports
    to Parliament. The principal formal reports to parliament
    include the Estimates, the Public Accounts and the Auditor
    General's Annual Report.

A   Attest and Authority - the expression of an opinion on
    financial statements and the verification of parliamentary
    and governmental authority for expenditures.

M   Management Control - an evaluation of the system of
    management information and controls, including the internal
    audit/evaluation/ review functions, so as to ensure there
    is due regard to economy and efficiency and that
    appropriate procedures to evaluate and report on programme
    effectiveness, where such are feasible, are in place and
    operating satisfactorily - in short, value for money auditir

E   EDP Controls - an evaluation of controls over financial
     and other information processed by computers and for
     management controls over the use of computer-related
     resources.

This acronym is useful in that it provides an overview, but

not one whose components slot easily together like so many

pieces in a jigsaw puzzle. Each description does though

illustrate the 'comprehensive' characteristics required by

this new approach to auditing. The emphasis is more directed

towards testing the effectiveness of procedures and practices

at all levels in the public sector.

A New Role

In adapting to this expanded role the auditor faces many

difficulties. There will be an increasing need for specialist

staff who will have to work with departmental management in

determining whether or not they and their staff have been

successful in producing the level and quantity of service

required by those who formulate policy. The role of the

auditor should be to support management by assisting in

pointing out deficiencies and advising on possible courses

of action. The auditor is not concerned with policy, but

with its effects and whether such effects correspond with

the intentions of the policy. This is a monitoring function,

a comparison of the situation that exists with that which

might have been expected.

The approach of the VFM audit should be essentially 'top-down'. The VFM audit should begin with a preliminary analysis of financial statistics and other performance indicators. Where trends or variations occur, these should be investigated. This would be done via a formalized internal structure, whereby senior management would liaise with the VFM auditors.

It may also be desirable for organization to have an internal VFM audit team and a VFM audit committee. At the same time there should be a review of the main organizational structure, the key policy objectives, and the major deployment of resources.

For each part of the organization it is then necessary to identify activities undertaken, and their purpose. An examination should be made of those outputs that are measurable and the costs involved: this information is needed to assess efficiency and effectiveness. The VFM auditor is concerned to see that planned activities have been achieved, and should not be involved in the setting of targets.

There is a strong relationship to more recent developments

in internal management systems such as planning programming

budgeting, and zero-based budgeting. Both techniques, being

programme-oriented, closely relate activity to the objectives

of an organization.

The conduct of the VFM audit should be flexible, and

obviously depends upon what the initial review reveals.

Ultimately the VFM audit becomes a regular and routine audit

process. If efficiency and effectiveness targets are based

on sound information, the final results should resemble

closely those predicted.

As the development of the VFM audit is in its infancy in

Britain, several problems have yet to be satisfactorily

resolved. The auditing profession must accept that it has

to broaden its horizons and develop techniques that have

hitherto been regarded as of academic interest only. If the

theory behind work processes change, then new techniques

must be developed.

Specialized assistance may need to be sought, and this may

mean that audit teams are no longer composed solely of

accountants. The VFM auditors will have to produce a

comprehensive report that is not only for the internal

consumption of management or elected officials, but is

available also to consumer councils and the general public.

Auditors must, therefore, ensure that adequate information

is provided for those that have a right of access to such

information.

Failure to meet these changing needs can only lead to an

undermining of the audit profession by critics who will

continue to question the value of the conventional audit

report for public sector organizations.

NOTES

1   Quoted in 'Value for Money Audits: Proceedings of a
      Seminar', Royal Institute of Public Administration,
      1982. (In association with Peat, Marwick, Mitchell &
      Co.)

2   Earlier reviews, such as The Plowden Committee on
      Public Expenditure (HMSO Cmnd 1432) had been more
      concerned with macro-economic management rather than
      our concern, management control.

3   Parliamentary Debates: Commons (Hansard), 1976-77,
      Vol. 922, p.661.

2
Economy And Efficiency Auditing

The phrase 'value for money' has a wide and often ambiguous

meaning. It is commonly used by the media when presenting

political arguments for expenditure cuts; particularly

when used in conjunction with other phrases such as 'cash

limits'. It is important to break this association and

instead present a more considered view on the objective of

attaining value for money from any organization. Holtham

and Stewart state (p. 3):

"We see the new concern as arising in an era of restraint,
but see that the case for value for money stands apart from
the political stance taken - whether it is for or against
cuts in local government expenditure. Value for money is
justified whatever level of expenditure is aimed at.
... Questions of value for money are about political
judgement - the judgement of what is value for money.
Value for money does not remove political judgement - it
may well increase the emphasis on it. We argue, however,
that the process of search for value for money is politically
neutral, even though what is decided in that process will
not be."

The last sentence of this quotation draws an important

distinction. The auditor is not concerned with policy,
which is the responsibility of elected politicians and
public servants who administer their directions. The
auditor is concerned with investigating the outcomes of
policy and whether such effects correspond with the intentions
of the policy. This is an apolitical monitoring function,
a comparison of the situation that exists with that which
might have been expected.

To say that a particular department (or programme) provides
value for money means that those who strive to provide the
service do so as best as they can, given the resources that
are available and the environment within which they operate.
It is impossible to provide an absolute measure of value for
money. The auditor must examine whether resources could be
put to alternative uses, whether objectives could be achieved
by an alternative strategy and (if practicable) compare the
operations of one particular department with another.

In 1972 a US Government Accounting Office publication (called
"the yellow book") acknowledged an expanded audit role within
the public sector. The yellow book defined the objectives
of auditing as reviewing:

(a)   financial operations and compliance with applicable laws and regulations

(b)   economy and efficiency of management practices, and

(c)   the effectiveness of programmes in achieving a desired level of results.

A decade later British auditors now face the same expanded responsibilities. As outlined in the opening chapter, three words have been introduced which, together, comprise the elements required when attesting value for money. These are now defined.[1]

ECONOMY: Acquiring resources of an appropriate quality for the minimum cost.

A lack of economy could occur, for example, when there is overstaffing; or when overqualified staff or overpriced facilities are used.

EFFICIENCY: Seeking to ensure that the maximum output is obtained from the resources devoted to a department (or programme), or alternatively, ensuring that only the minimum level of resources are devoted to a given level of output.

An operation could be said to have increased in efficiency
if either fewer inputs were used to produce a given amount
of output, or a given level of input resulted in increased
output. Inefficiency would be revealed by identifying the
performance of work with no useful purpose, or the accumulation
of an excess of (or un-necessary) material and supplies.

EFFECTIVENESS: Ensuring that the output from any given activity
                is achieving the desired results.

To evaluate effectiveness we need to establish that
approved/desired goals are being achieved. This is not
necessarily a straightforward procedure; some goals may
not be initially apparent. Once a set of goals has been
established we need to examine whether these goals are
being accomplished.

These elements have been ranked in order of comprehensibility
and measurability, although they are clearly interrelated
to one another. In more detail:

To establish economy of operation means to examine the
organization's internal regulations for the creation of
standards, establishments etc.

It may be that independent support for certain of these

arrangements can be, and should be, sought. Typically, areas

for the examination of economy would include inspection of

national agreements on pay, staffing and so forth; professional

guidelines; Organisations and Methods reports; and technical

specifications. Once quality of resources is established,

the auditor would then need to establish that they were

obtained at minimum cost, perhaps more aptly described as

'acceptable' in relation to local conditions of operation.

This last point may be important. For example, if there

was a shortage of a particular specialist or grade of

staff it may only be possible to employ someone who is

over rather than under-skilled.

Efficiency is harder to verify. The definition implies that

we can measure output per unit of input, but this may not be

so easily quantified. Some government departments could

perhaps provide relevant statistics. For example, the

National Health Service has figures for bed occupancy and

the treatment of certain categories of patients. Other

organizations would need to develop appropriate/relevant

measures. A local authority's cleansing department could

provide figures for dustbins emptied, miles of footpaths

and roads swept etc.

Such guidelines could be nationally agreed to aid

comparability between segments or divisions of each

organization. Though desirable one would need to establish

safeguards. To continue with our local authority illustration,

a distinction would have to be made between the activities

of rural and urban authorities. A useful comparison could

perhaps be made between a local authority in Devon and

another in the Yorkshire Dales, but neither could be compared

with the GLC. Output measures need to be relevant, agreed

and implemented by management (and unions); and capable of

measurement. In any comparison, cost differences themselves

are fairly meaningless: it is the underlying reasons for

such differences that are important.

Effectiveness involves an examination of the relationship

between the output and objectives of the department. The

auditor has the task of deciding whether predetermined

goals are being achieved. Effectiveness indicates whether

results have been achieved, irrespective of the resources

used to achieve those results. It could be that effectiveness

could be obtained more efficiently.

A conflict can arise between efficiency and effectiveness.

For example, the ratepayer is on the one hand concerned

with the efficiency of the sevices he or she receives from

the local authority. On the other hand, he or she is

concerned about the level of contribution required.

As Hepworth states (p.239):

"The conflict between efficiency and effectiveness,
particularly in sensitive services like education and
social services, is extremely difficult to resolve, and is
left to individual judgements, which really means the
judgement of those most concerned with the development of
the service."

The auditor must determine the reasonableness of these

individual judgements. As previously stated it may be

that specialist (non-accounting) assistance will need

to be sought.

Assessing the effectiveness of programmes in achieving a

desired level of results is the newest and most difficult

area of work that the auditor has to adapt to. For this

reason the whole of Chapter 3 is devoted to this element.

Appendices B and C provide checklists, one on operations

and the other on spending, which can be examined to see

their present operation and possible future in the promotion

of value for money.

Using Auditing To Improve Efficiency

Efficiency, as outlined above, refers to the productive use

of resources. In order to produce efficiency measures we

need to identify and measure both programme outputs and

inputs so that we can measure how well the available resources

are being used. The purpose of attempting to define efficiency

measures involves arriving at an assessment of the following:[2]

(a)   the suitable delineation of individual departmental

      or programme goals to all levels of the organization;

(b)   the adequacy of controls and systems used by management

      in monitoring and measuring both the efficiency and

      level of service that they offer;

(c)   the present level of efficiency currently attained,

      as well as measures of comparable results (if available);

(d)   the efforts taken to improve methods of operation in

      order to improve efficiency;

(e)   whether efficiency measures are feasible, and if not

      the reasons why.

Sven Ivor Ivarson (p.7) stresses the need for administration

to translate goals into operational terms. In order to be

able to carry out a systematic evaluation of an organization's

activities there is the prime need for systematic and programme

planning. Ivarson believes that, although organizations have

vertical lines of communication, the evaluation of programme

efficiency (and for that matter effectiveness) must be done

horizontally. This is because management, depending on
their position within the organization, will have different
responsibilities and receive different kinds of data. It
follows that since it is the role of management that the
auditor is evaluating, the criteria which the auditor
selects must be appropriate to each level of management.
VFM reports should be fairly detailed, with individual
sections that refer to the responsibilities of particular
line managers together with an overall summary for senior
officials, elected representatives etc.

The Audit Guide on Efficiency produced by the office of the
Auditor General of Canada draws an important distinction between
efficiency and productivity. The terms are often used (though
quite wrongly) as synonyms for each other. The guide (p.2)
states:

> "- Productivity is the arithmetical ratio between the
>   amount of goods or services produced and the amount
>   of resources used in the course of production -
>   the ratio between output and input.
> - Efficiency is the relationship of actual output/input
>   (productivity) to a performance standard. This
>   relationship is usually expressed as a percentage."

The efficiency of an operation should therefore be compared
to a predetermined standard or target. Efficiency can be
measured in terms of the rate of return of production, the

work content measured over time, or the unit cost of an

output. Consider the following example in relation to the

dispensing of prescriptions by a hospital pharmacy.

Example. A hospital employs two pharmacists who each work

a 35-hour week. The standard rate of production is

6 prescriptions/hour; which in terms of work content in

time is 10 minutes/prescription. Each pharmacist is paid

£5.10 per hour so that the unit cost per prescription is

85p. Figures show that on average 1,848 prescriptions are

dispensed by one pharmacist each month. Efficiency can be

measured as follows:

(a) $\dfrac{\text{Actual rate per hour}}{\text{Standard rate per hour}} \quad = \dfrac{6.60 \text{ prescriptions}}{6 \text{ prescriptions}} \times 100 = 110\%$

of Efficiency.

(b) $\dfrac{\text{Standard time per prescription}}{\text{Actual time per prescription}} = \dfrac{10 \text{ minutes}}{9.09 \text{ minutes}} \times 100 = 110\%$

of Efficiency.

(c) $\dfrac{\text{Standard Cost per prescription}}{\text{Actual cost per prescription}} = \dfrac{85p}{77p} \times 100 = 110\% \text{ of}$

Efficiency.

Various points arise from this simple example. In comparing

actual costs with standard costs the auditor has first to

consider the economy of operations. Efficiency measures
are only possible when outputs can be separated from each
other and possess uniform characteristics. A repetitive
process, as in our example, meets these criteria. There
are instances when efficiency measures are either not
practicable or not possible. An example could be a
community police programme. Though tasks may be clearly
stated (school visiting, crime prevention enquiries, contact
with ethnic minorities etc.) outputs, not being tangible,
cannot be measured.

When an agreed standard of performance does not exist it
might be useful to compare present performance with some
previous base period (e.g. the same month last year).
Such a base period output/input ratio is termed an historical
standard or target. This assumes that past performance is
indicative of future performance and this may not always
be so. If a new service is building up a clientele base
then one could naturally expect the efficiency ratio to
improve over time.

A useful list of comparison measures was provided by Hatry
et al for the Urban Institute, Washington D.C.[3]

"1.   Comparisons over time.
 2.   Measurements compared between geographical areas.

3. Comparison of actual performance with <u>standards</u>
    particularly in relation to standardized procedures.
4. Comparison of actual performance with performance
    <u>targeted</u> at the beginning of the year.
5. Comparison with similar <u>private sector</u> activities.
6. <u>Inter-authority</u> comparisons."

Efficiency should not be measured for efficiency's sake;

improving efficiency is the objective. By developing

efficiency measures management can contribute to improving

it and to determining the expected gains from suggested

improvements. Concern by management to monitor efficiency

should serve to focus regular attention on the subject

rather than attract ad hoc attention as suggested in

Chapter 1.

The 1981 Canadian Audit Guide (p.5) discussed the importance

of efficiency measures in the following terms:

"Standards and performance data are used for different
purposes in various information and control systems.
These are to:

- demonstrate achievement of results by comparing performance
  data to standards, targets and goals;

- plan operations and budget resource requirements by
  providing data for comparing present and proposed methods
  and procedures;

- provide a rational basis for pricing goods and services
  (when charges are made);[4]

- make trade-off decisions between efficiency and the level
  of service; and

- indicate to employees and supervisors what results are expected. (Therefore, standards are useful both in appraising the performance of managers and groups of employees and in motivating them.)"

The key elements for management that therefore arise from

adopting efficiency measures are:

(a)   an awareness of, and the determination to accomplish, programme goals in the most economical and efficient manner;

(b)   the need to plan operations as efficiently as possible for a given level of resources (or budgeted level of income if a statutory authority is expected to largely generate its own income);

(c)   the need to have a structured organization whose administration should follow prescribed work measures and procedures in order to avoid duplicaiton of effort, unnecessary tasks, idle time etc.; and

(d)   the provision of work instructions, in sufficient detail, to employees who are suitably qualified and trained for the duties they are required to perform.

The auditor's role is to satisfy himself or herself that

management are 'geared up' to tackle the goals that they

have been set. The audit criteria used by the office of

the Auditor General of Canada were first published in its

1978 annual report;[5] these were:

(a)   Measures of performance should be relevant and accurate.

(b)   Performance should be adequate in comparison to a standard.

(c)   Reports should be tailored to management's needs.

(d)   Productivity data should be used to achieve
       productivity improvements.

(e)   Productivity measures and reports should be kept
       current.

In measuring performance the characteristics of the output,

such as quality and level of service should be clearly

stated. Audit reports should endeavour to comment on the

appropriateness of the indicators used. The auditor would

have to decide, possibly with the aid of specialist advice,

what was a reasonable level of tolerance in deciding whether

certain activities warranted an exception report. The

third point on this list relates to the need to evaluate

programmes horizontally, as previously discussed. The

audit report should be designed to aid management's efforts

by reporting on matters that require attention. Of necessity

a VFM audit can only examine segments of an organization

at any one time. Areas for investigation will be the

subject of negotiation between senior management and the

auditor but the details of the audit investigation will

involve discussions with those at an operational level.

The auditor would also wish to see evidence that performance

data was used to plan budget allocations and that performance

measurement systems should be modified as necessary to

reflect programme changes arising because of management

direction or from new legislation.

The auditor is called upon to report upon any symptoms of inefficiency that arise. Various indicators might indicate inefficiency. It may be that an historical trend indicates a disproportionate growth in resources used in comparison to growth in the level of service provided. The auditor may conclude that the efficiency measurement system adopted produces biased results or that performance should be measured in situations that it currently is not. There could be a high rate of customer or client complaints, an excessive backlog of work or failure to exploit obvious opportunities which would lead to improved efficiency.

Figure 2 was designed by the Canadian Office of the Auditor General to provide an overview of an efficiency audit.

It is the first responsibility of management to ensure that their present mode of operation and work procedures are as efficient as possible given the prevailing conditions, level of funding and available technology. Management should constantly review procedures in order to improve productivity. It is the auditors' role to confirm that management carries out this responsibility.

The Need For Appropriate Statistics and Comparative Studies

To date most of the work in developing statistics useful to

Figure 2   Schematic overview of an efficiency audit

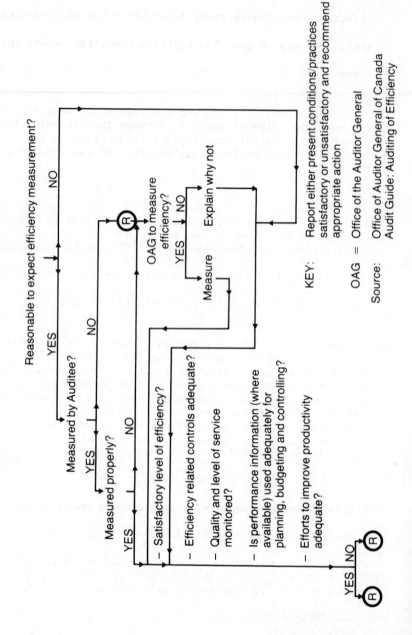

KEY: Report either present conditions/practices
           satisfactory or unsatisfactory and recommend
           appropriate action

OAG = Office of the Auditor General

Source: Office of Auditor General of Canada
           Audit Guide: Auditing of Efficiency

the VFM auditor has been carried out in the field of Local

Government. There are also pilot projects in the Health

Service to provide relevant information but this work has

still some way to go. The Layfield Committee report (p.95)

states that

"...the best way of promoting efficiency and securing value
for money by external means is through the dissemination
of comprehensive but intelligible information on the
methods employed by local authorities and the results they
achieve."

This view was supported in the First Report of the Advisory

Committee on Local Government Audit (The Maynard Committee).

Published in July 1980, four years after the report of the

Layfield Committee, this report stated (p.12):

"We support this view and consider that one of the most
effective means of securing these objectives is the
widespread use of comparative studies. We have therefore
been concerned to find that many local authorities have
yet to recognize such studies as useful aids to management,
and that more progress has not been made in developing a
coordinated approach to the forms such studies should
take, who should undertake them, and how such results
should be published."

Whilst the wider adoption of such studies needs to be

undertaken by many more local authorities, it is true to

say that for the major part of the total Government

expenditure no similar information is available.

Comparative statistics do have important advantages but their use also needs to be tempered by the recognition that such statistics also have their limitations. The following points, adapted from those suggested by the Maynard Committee, relate to local authorities but are equally applicable in other spheres of the public sector.

ADVANTAGES:

(a)   Comparative statistics provide a basis for the interchange of information useful in determining the costs and peformance of comparable local authority functions.

(b)   They may indicate that long established policies and practices may be in need of review since other authorities follow different practices that should be investigated in order to improve upon economy and efficiency.

(c)   Such information is relatively inexpensive to obtain and is therefore a useful guide for indicating areas for detailed investigation.

DISADVANTAGES:

(a)   Statistics in themselves do not provide positive

indications of efficiency or inefficiency. The fact
that one authority is spending more on social welfare
programmes than other authorities are does not mean
that such programmes are inefficient or uneconomical.
It could be that this particular authority has acute
social and/or environmental factors that also need
to be considered.

(b)   Efficiency measures in isolation are no guide to
       effectiveness - see Chapter 3.

(c)   Some local authorities fear that central government
       may use such information either to promote uniform
       spending or to redistribute funds.

(d)   Variations in costs may be due, in part to the adoption
       of different accounting practices.

Besides local authorities producing their own statistics
(often used in their published accounts as supplementary
information), information is compiled by professional
bodies such as the Chartered Institute of Public Finance
and Accountancy (CIPFA) or the District Auditors' Society's
Statistical Information Service. CIPFA is the largest
provider of information with some thirty-one separate

volumes provided by its finacial information service as
well as its annual statistics (based on the estimates
produced by local authorities in England and Wales) which
are grouped under twenty-one headings.

Summary comparative studies on VFM audits and investigations
are now also becoming available. The most widely known are
those produced, again, by CIPFA and also by the Local
Authorities Management Services and Computer Committee
(LAMSAC). Each entry generally indicates the type of
local aauthority; the department or service reviewed;
the subject/programme investigated; a brief description
of the objectives of the work undertaken and the techniques
used; and a summary of the results obtained.

Individual local authorities have undertaken some useful
research in an effort to improve the quality of information
for performance measurement. Mention is made of two such
studies. The first was published by Epping Forest District
Council in 1976, whilst the second was published by Basildon
Council in 1981.

(a)   'Performance Measurement in Local Government: A
        Report of a Study of Five District Councils'.

Epping Forest District Council obtained the co-operation of

four other adjacent District Councils for this project.
The process of performance measures between these five
councils followed three stages: (i) the identification
and quantification of inputs and outputs;   (ii) the
weighting of the different outputs so as to enable them to
be related and counted together; and (iii) the division of
the weighted output by input to produce a performance
indicator.

Weighted outputs could have been divided by any one of a
number of inputs to produce the performance indicator but
only two were chosen - employee costs and man-years. The
authors of this report made this selection because wages
and salaries were regarded as an important controllable
resource accounting for about 70% of revenue expenditure.
The criteria adopted to identify outputs were that (i)
they should be final outputs of the organization;   (ii)
they should be quantifiable;   (iii) they should so far as
possible reflect the aims and objectives of the council or
department;   and (iv) they should not motivate management
in the wrong way. The outputs identified were discussed
with staff and two levels of final outputs were identified
- operational outputs, which are the final outputs of
departments, and programme outputs which are the final
outputs of the authority as a whole. The bases of weighting

used were: the unit cost base weight and the man-year
base weight.

(b)   'A Classification of English Non-Metropolitan Districts
        - A simple analysis of English Non-Metropolitan
        District Councils, to assist in the selection of
        comparators.'

The idea behind this study was to provide divisions of local
authorities against which individual local authorities could
compare their performance.   The data used in the analysis was
a subset taken from that used by the Department of the
Environment in calculating the grant-related expenditure
component for the 1981/82 Rate Support Grant Settlements.
Unlike other cluster studies, this one did not wholly rely
upon socio-econonomic data, and was simply based on ten
succinct variables which were given equal statistical
weighting.   The variables used to group similar authorities
were: (i) daytime population; (ii) elderly dependency
ratio;   (iii) youth dependency ratio; (iv) population
growth;   (v) domestic contribution;   (vi) capital
allocations; (vii) housing density;   (viii) council housing
stock;   (ix) housing/social conditions factor;   and
(x) rebate ratio.   This process grouped all of the local
authorities in England and Wales into fifteen divisions.

Both of these local authorities are to be commended for
sponsoring this valuable work. The first study enabled
five local authorities to examine and compare output,
input and performance indices. The results enabled council
officers and a review team to make enquiries into the more
significant differences. For example, for output 4 (Pools
and Sports Centres) District Council A's relatively low
performance was explained by the greater number of swimming
pools in relation to the population. The authority took
steps to rationalize the opening hours at various pools.
In the second study authorities were able to locate suitable
other non-metropolitan districts if they wished to monitor
their performance. Included in Group 6, for example, were
West Derby, West Devon and East Cambridge.

Case Study I: An Economy and Efficiency Audit

The idea for this case study was provided by Audit Standard
Supplement Series, No.7, 'Using Auditing to Improve
Efficiency and Economy', produced by The Department of The
Controller General of The United States.

The external auditor of the Barchester District Council has
been examining the available management information (provided
from such sources as budgets, departmental reports, and annual

reports). As a result of these deliberations he discusses
various areas of concern which both he and senior officers
of the authority agree require further investigation. One
area selected for an economy and efficiency review is the
Vehicle Maintenance Department. This is a service department
providing maintenance for all the authority's vehicles:
motor cars, light commercial vehicles, heavy commercial
vehicles and a variety of special purpose vehicles. The
last category includes road sweepers, refuse trucks, grass
cutting tractors and attachments, etc.

The budget for the present year, 1983/84, was £350,000 for
this department. Already half-way through the year
(30 September) there was a deficit to date of £34,000.
The auditor began his work by gathering information and
trying to 'narrow down' the department's activities into a
few areas manageable enough to audit. The object of this
initial exercise was to find out what the department did,
how it was staffed, who did what, and what information was
available. A tour was also organized to enable the auditor
and his staff to get a 'feel' for the physical layout of
the department and to take a first hand look at what it
did. As the investigation continued there were further
'follow-up' interviews with some of the supervisors and
additional information was gathered. The following five

examples illustrate the many different approaches that
were used to identify and develop upon ideas that eventually
formed the basis of the final report.

1.   Using Available Data

The departmental manager had a useful system of record
cards which recorded all details of regular maintenance
and repairs carried out on each vehicle. He agreed that
there were too many different makes of motor cars and
light commercial vehicles used by the authority. This
meant that a larger than necessary level of stock had to
be kept as many routine replacement parts were not compatible.
He also agreed that the authority had no proper replacement
procedure (see 2). Both of these points arose because
individual departments decided their vehicle requirements
and made acquisition proposals through their respective
committees without seeking advice from the Vehicle
Maintenance Manager.

By purchasing vehicles from an approved list the savings in
spare parts stock was estimated at £6,000. Over time there
would also be an improvement in efficiency since certain
maintenance jobs would become more standard. The benefit
from this was not costed.

2.   Observation

On a return visit to the department the auditor questioned

a supervisor about some major work being carried out on a

lightweight commercial delivery van. The supervisor

stated that the van was six years old and had nearly 100,000

miles on the clock. The work was necessary as otherwise

the vehicle would fail an imminent road-worthiness test.

As referred to under point 1, individual departments had

total discretion over their vehicle requirements and there

was no universal replacement policy. The work on this

particular van was costed at £650 (i.e. labour and materials

only) whilst its market value was probably of the order of

£500. Both the supervisor and the departmental manager

agreed that such repair work was not an isolated incident.

With the aid of these two men providing estimates of

maintenance, safety checks etc., the auditor was able to

draw up a suggested replacement policy based on the economic

life of each vehicle rather than its physical life. The

savings in this department were estimated at £40,000 per

annum, and this was slightly offset by additional capital

costs to give an estimated net saving to the authority of

£32,000 per annum. About half of these savings in the

department represented the wages of two fitters. The

manager agreed that this element of savings could be met

by not replacing the positions vacated by two men who were

due to retire within the next twelve months.

3.   The Supervisors' Schedule

The audit team found that, generally, there was no ordered

routine to the supervisors' duties. Eight supervisors

covered a variety of tasks: mechanical, electrical, paint-

spraying, panel beating and so on. The supervisors

complained that there just was not enought time to do the

things they thought needed more attention, such as giving

more time to work scheduling, conducting cost studies and

looking at new equipment that they had heard about.

Close examination revealed that on occasions the supervisors

duplicated some of the duties of their chargehands. By

streamlining some of the paperwork involved, including

involving the storeman (who was under-utilized) in collating

some of the paperwork, additional time was saved. This

led to a saving of two posts, or £18,000 per annum.

4.   A Combination Approach

By a combination of direct observation and an examination

of job cards further savings were identified. For example,

refuse collection trucks required regular oil changes for
their hydraulic gear. Whilst mileage was low for these
vehicles they were continually grinding down rubbish.
This work was usually done on a Saturday morning so as to
have these vehicles ready for use on the Monday morning.
The daily shifts of the maintenance men and the refuse
collectors was such that each afternoon these vehicles
were returned to their depot one and a half hours before
the maintenance department closed. Rescheduling removed
the need for Saturday working which was all paid on overtime.
This single instance saved £9,000 per annum and the total
savings under this category of exercise amounted to almost
£15,000 per annum.

5.   Ideas From Past Studies

A good source of information in any organization is its
file of study reports, whether conducted internally or by
consultants. The audit team became aware of an earlier
internal report which examined the authority's requirements
for office space, workshops and storage facilities. This
earlier report had recommended that a former primary school
site could be used to accommodate this department plus two
storage yards belonging to the Building and Maintenance
Department and the Highways Department. This earlier report

had not been implemented as the school site was not at that

time zoned as an industrial area. Recently, however, the

site had been reclassified by the County Council. The

audit team reviewed and concurred with the earlier

recommendations and updated the costings which were now

three years out of date. After allowing for capital outlay

and receipts from the sale of the three present sites

there was a net once-and-for-all gain to the authority of

approximately £185,000 with annual savings in operating

costs of £46,000. Of the operating figure, about £12,000

related to the Vehicle Maintenance Costs. The development

would provide improved working conditions for the staff

and was expected to lead to greater efficiency.

Excluding the development outlined under point 5, which

would take two years to develop, the other savings would

save the authority approximately £70,000 per annum.

The points to note from this case study are as follows:

(a)   Both the auditor and senior officers selected areas

       for investigation. Whilst the auditor may well have

       programmes that, independently, he has decided to

       investigate; it is useful for management if their

       suggestions can, on occasion, also be included.

(b)   At all times, the departmental manager and supervisors
       were informed of developments and indeed contributed
       positively to various parts of the investigation.

(c)   As will be further discussed in Chapter 4, the final
       report was discussed, at draft stage, with the
       departmental manager who could then comment before
       the final draft was submitted to Council Members.

Note also that the audit team did not recommend the use of
performance indicators as there was no uniformity in the
output from this department.

Notes

1.   These definitions were developed whilst on secondment
       to Price Waterhouse UK and are now also to be found
       in their auditing manual entitled 'Value for Money',
       1982.

2.   Adapted from 'Audit Guide: Auditing of Efficiency',
       the office of the Auditor General of Canada, 1981.

3.   Also quoted in Holtham and Stewart, p.17.

4.   This reference is really only appropriate to government
       departments and agencies and statutory authorities that
       charge for their services.

5.   Each of these headings was followed by several paragraphs
       outlining the application(s) required.

3
Effectiveness Auditing

In these opening paragraphs we briefly consider why there
is a need for independent, informed and unbiased comment
on the effectiveness of the programmes undertaken by
government departments and agencies.

Politicians and administrators should clearly be interested
in the effectiveness of the programmes with which they are
most directly concerned. Much of the comments made by these
two groups, on the impact of particular programmes, is based
on neither reliable nor valid information. Indeed the
public seem to expect those committed to a particular
service to extol its virtues. Statements to the effect
that a particular programme has had an increase in funding
do not say anything about the quality of the service offered.
Neither does a statement such as: "there will be no increase
in postal charges in the next six months."

The public, as clients, equally base their attitudes on the

quality of the services they receive, on subjective

assessments that are more than a little conditioned by

their individual social attitudes. What one might term

'topical' programmes, such as the general quality of health

care, the price of electricity, the level of defence

expenditure, and so on, receive wide publicity. By contrast,

little attention is given to lesser funded 'acute' programmes

such as those for the mentally ill, drug addiction and the

provision of overseas aid.

Whoever is the commentator, opinions expressed are often

only belief, based on sketchy information that is only

indirectly relevant.

Programme evaluation, through effectiveness auditing, is

measuring the extent to which goals have been attained.

The goals are the aims or outcomes that a programme purports

to pursue and for which it can be held accountable (where

measurable). Programme evaluation is more than an

examination of the manner in which a programme is implemented.

It should also review the results achieved. The aim of

the auditor should be to link programme processes; for

example, the number of children receiving a particular

immunization vaccination should be linked to the outcome,

here possibly expressed in terms of a decrease in a

particular illness or infirmity. Such analysis can provide
useful and constructive information which can guide
politicians and administrators in making programme
improvements as well as provide a reasonably objective
assessment on behalf of the public at large. In some
instances it may be possible to produce quantitative data
to support recommendations; in other instances it may be
provided by the perceived value of a service based on a
consumer survey.

Generally, before a programme is introduced or expanded,
some form of analysis is undertaken on which the policy
decision is based (an ex ante evaluation). Such analysis
can be based upon a variety of approaches, some more
scientific than others, such as needs assessment, cost-
benefit studies, management by objectives, planned programme
budgeting systems (PPBS), zero-based budgeting and so on.
Many of these are new tools designed to provide a systematic
framework within which the political and management process
can operate. For example, where a form of programme
budgeting has been adopted it has meant that budgetary
requests are made for specified programme activities rather
than by the traditional block allocation approach. Such
new developments are not without their critics, though this
is not the appropriate forum to enter this debate.[1]

However, defects aside, what does appear clear is that the object of such evaluations is to help clarify goals as well as to question the assumptions, often taken for granted, which usually underlie the implementation or continuation of certain programmes. Effectiveness auditing provides the ex post review of previous policy decisions.

For on-going projects, the reports prepared by the auditor should be seen as iterative in the sense that findings and recommendations are passed on to management to enable adjustments to be made for the future improvement of services. One understandable fear of line management, not so much with the notion of accountability, is that such investigations will be misused and lead to programmes being curtailed or reduced. This is because most programmes, viewed in isolation, provide a limited response to often long-standing and complex problems. For example, it would not be proper for an effectiveness audit to consider distributional and value questions as to what programmes ought to be provided and for whom.

Every investigation will inevitably have to be tailored to local operating conditions. There cannot be an overall standard approach. The auditor's role is to direct the attention of those responsible for devising and initiating policy. He is not directly concerned with the solution of problems, otherwise he becomes responsible for those solutions and thereby loses his objectivity and status to provide an independent examination and appraisal of a service. It is management that has to address itself to the solutions, either by using internal resources or by engaging outside consultants.

Each investigation should conclude with an independent assessment by the auditor of the problems that exist and the changes required. Very often the auditor reports to two levels - to operational management and to central administration. Such reports serve two purposes:

(a)   To provide Parliament, government and the public with an independent analysis which can serve as a basis for questioning those responsible and establishing future priorities and direction of activities.

(b)   To provide decision-makers in the activity examined with ideas about how they could promote effectiveness.

Careful planning of the investigation and well drafted reporting both discussed with all management levels should avoid fears of misuse.

Effectiveness auditing is a rather wide concept that is primarily concerned with three aspects:[2]

Goal Analysis - the ability of operating departments to translate the intentions of parliament and government into operational goals.

Audit of Operations - examining whether output corresponds to required need and whether resources have been optimally deployed.

Audit of Systems - ensuring that a department plans, manages and evaluates its various operations, and implements indicated changes.

The auditor has to review the effects of policy as determined and initiated by both central and devolved Government departments - in effect to answer the question: has a particular department interpreted its duties in line with the intentions of central administration?

Assessing Effectiveness

The initial planning by the auditor is all important to the way in which the investigation is conducted. He must be careful not to carry out 'black-box' evaluations, which being narrow in perception produce narrow assessments. Rutman (1980) succintly summarizes the initial approach that should be made by the auditor before undertaking an

effectiveness audit (p.36):

"The first general concern of the evaluability assessment
is to determine the extent to which the program is
structured to make it amenable to an evaluation of its
effectiveness. The aim is to identify those program
components and goal/effects that should be considered for
inclusion in an evaluation. The following questions are
central: Is the program (or its components) clearly defined
and capable of being implemented in a prescribed manner?
Are the goals and effects clearly specified? Can the
program realistically achieve the specified goals or produce
the anticipated effects? Procedures of analyzing the
program to answer these questions include: reviews of
program documents, interviews and collecting information in
the field.

The second general concern is determining the feasibility
of conducting an evaluation to meet the study's purposes.
The important questions include: what is the purpose of
the evaluation? What are the methodological requirements?
Can the program be designed and implemented to meet evaluation
requirements? Is there an accepted methodology that can be
used for the study? What limitations and restrictions are
 placed on the study by the various constraints - financial,
legal, ethical, and administrative?"

It is useful at the planning stage for the auditor to orient

himself by examining the history of the department or agency

and to familiarize himself with its organizational strucure.

He should be familiar with all relevant legislation and regulations.

Programmes should be identified as well as their effectiveness

measurement systems. It is the appropriateness of this system

that will determine the review strategy. This overview approach

is particularly important when the scope of the engagement

is broad and the time-scale limited. The auditor can then

determine how best to allocate the time of his team so that

they can produce significant findings and recommendations.

The most critical requirement of an effectiveness audit is

a clear statement of the programme objectives for which the

level of achievement is to be measured. The client should

identify those objectives as a matter of course in the

relevant engagement documentation. Indeed, such documentation

should make reference to the source of these objectives;

for example, enabling legislation or ministerial direction.

The importance of this requirement can be appreciated from

the following passage taken from the United States General

Accounting Office's Exposure Draft 'Comprehensive Approach

For Planning and Conducting A Program Results Review'

(p.21):

"The lack of an objective set of standards or principles to
govern effectiveness measurement systems creates the
potential for two unique problems that may affect the
conduct of a program results review assignment. Although
these problems may never surface, they should be anticipated
and the methods for resolving the potential problems should
be clarified before beginning the review. These potential
problems involve:

- Irreconcilable differences between the review staff and
  program management over the appropriateness of the system
  used to measure effectiveness.

- Contingent work responsibilities that are not readily
  identifiable before preparing the work plan or bid proposal.

The subjective nature of measuring program effectiveness may
lead to irreconcilable differences between the review staff

and program management. The appropriateness of specific
performance indicators, data sources and performance
standards is determined primarily by their relationship is
not always precise. In the absence of such precision,
reasonable approximations may be considered. Reasonableness,
however, is a subjective judgement, which in turn can lead
to differences of opinion...".

On this last point, three solutions are possible: (i) the

conflict is passed to a higher authority; (ii) the auditor,

as the independent assessor, is granted the authority to

assert and defend whatever position he believes appropriate;

or (iii) no further work is done and the VFM audit is

restricted to only two elements - economy and efficiency.

Whatever the solution, it should be resolved prior to the

commencement of the review.

It is for the auditor to decide whether it is appropriate

to proceed with an effectiveness audit once this planning/

assessment stage is completed. There may be many reasons

that lead the auditor to conclude that he should not proceed.

It could be that a programme has only just commenced, or

that its operations have been recently revised, and that a

longer review period is thought desirable. There could be

a conflict, not as mentioned in the previous paragraph,

but rather due to the impreciseness of the programme

objectives. Politicians can often be accused of deliberately

designing vague legislation due to the inevitable need to

reach a compromise position. This helps neither administrators nor auditors.

The next stage in an effectiveness audit is that of review. If the auditor is satisfied with the adequacy of the management's system of effectiveness measurement (or monitoring) he can concentrate his attention on the reliability of their performance reports. Otherwise he will have to develop his own, ad hoc, system of measurement. We consider each approach in turn.

In order to examine the reliability of the management's performance reports, the auditor must: (i) document management's system for measuring effectiveness; (ii) assess the appropriateness of their performance indicators; (iii) verify the results obtained and compare with appropriate standards; and (iv) determine effectiveness based on management's systems.

Performance indicators will not be those developed to measure efficiency. For example, a Government regional development grant programme, for the redeployment of industry to economically depressed areas, should not be assessed in terms of effectiveness by the number of firms that relocate or by the total amount of grants paid. These are efficiency

measures only. One could only determine, from such measures,
the success (in work-load terms) of management in attracting
firms to move location. To measure effectiveness, the
auditor would have to use surrogate measures, such as the
improvement in the unemployment statistics in those areas.
There is no guide to the appropriate number of indicators
required to determine effectiveness. The use of multiple
indicators will increase the cost of the audit and additional
indicators should only be used if they materially improve
the measurement of results.

If the performance indicators used by management are
deficient the auditor should discuss this fact with
management and agree appropriate modifications. Very
often effectiveness can only be indicated by personal
opinions or judgement. To avoid bias such information
should either be obtained from independent third parties
or from client surveys.

An ad hoc system for measuring effectiveness is used by
the auditor either when management has no effectiveness
measurement system or when, upon examination, it is found
to be defective. If this is the case the auditor must
design the system and collect the data, making allowances
for any deficiencies he encounters. For example, consider

the problems of measuring the effectiveness of a Government
retraining programme if records fail to monitor the progress
of past trainees. The auditor might decide to survey past
trainees in order to find out whether they were currently
employed in a position that utilizes their new skills.
The problem is that the response rate may not be high
enough to provide a statistically significant answer.

When reviewing effectiveness, the auditor has to be mindful
of the fact that, despite the relevance of the performance
measures he has chosen, performance may be inhibited by
external factors. The effect of externalities on the
evaluation process depends on the extent that they could
have been avoided. Reconsider our retraining programme.
Let us suppose that management did have an adequate
monitoring system, one that was able to indicate that
those with certain specialisms were less likely than others
to obtain suitable employment. From the auditor's viewpoint
he would expect management to revise their plans; to close
down certain courses and expand others. If instead it was
found that industry itself was taking on the task of
retraining operatives with firms operating 'in-house'
courses, the auditor might conclude that the Government
scheme should be either drastically reduced or curtailed.

The final stage of the review is to summarize, discuss and report upon the results obtained from the performance measures used and determine whether the programme is achieving results that are compatible with its stated objectives. If effectiveness cannot be determined then the auditor should outline in his report the reasons that prevent its measurement. Alternatively, if a programme is not achieving a desired level of results, the report should identify the causes that prevent effective performance.

The assessment of effectiveness outlined above follows the approach adopted by both the United States General Accounting Office (GAO) and the Office of the Auditor General of Canada. The GAO identifies the following six stages for an effectiveness audit:

(a)   Pre-Review familiarization and planning activities;

(b)   Assessing management's effectiveness measurement system;

(c)   Using an ad hoc system to measure effectiveness;

(d)   Identifying causes that inhibit programme effectiveness;

(e)   Obtaining supplemental information;

(f)   Communicating the review findings.

Appendix D reproduces a comprehensive flowchart, developed by the GAO, to outline each of these stages.

A useful approach to VFM auditing has been developed by
the City of Thunder Bay, Ontario, Canada. The city is
committed to the advancement of modern management system
and performance measurement. In 1980 the city's Chief
Administrative Officer received the International City
Management's Innovation Award for Organization and
Management. The city's Corporate Planning and Development
Divison have categorized performance measures into three
groups:

(a) workload/demand measures: to indicate the amount of work
    done or to be done;
(b) efficiency measures: to measure how well resources are
    utilized; and
(c) effectiveness measures: to measure how well a goal or
    objective is being achieved.

Under this system each department is divided into programme
areas and a detailed programme description is provided.
The performance measures are provided under each category
together with details of the source of the information;
how it is to be collected; how it is to be analyzed
(manual/computer); and the frequency of data collection
(which ranges from annually to daily). Each programme is
discussed with the responsible manager and agreed by him.

One department covered by this exercise was that of Social

Services. Four of the programmes identified were: adult

services; child day care centres; field eligibility; and

hostels and crisis homes. The information provided on the

fourth of these programmes was as follows:[3]

Programme Description

To provide temporary living accommodation

for transient, unhouseable clients, problem male youths and

mothers in crisis.

Performance measurements	Source and how collected	How options Analyzed
(a) Workload/demand		
No. of clients serviced by programme & by caseworker	Internal records	Manual
No. of days service provided per programme	"	"
No. of days of occupancy of Crisis Homes	"	"
No. of Crisis Homes	"	"

(b) Efficiency measures		
Gross and net cost per day service by programme	Approved budget, and internal records	"

(c)　　Effectiveness measurements

| Occupancy percentage for all crisis homes and per home | Internal Records | " |
| Pecentage of eligible clients served by programme | " " | " " |

All data to be collected monthly by the department's own staff.

Citizen Surveys

One of the problems faced by Government service departments
and agencies is their inability to get a balanced and
comprehensive view of their clients' attitudes to the
services they provide. At present there is limited feedback
(via individuals, consumer groups and the media etc.)
which does not lend itself to a systematic examination.
Further, such views that are obtained may not be representative
of the entire population. Scientifically conducted surveys,
however, offer a unique means for either administration or
the auditor to obtain feedback on the quality of the services
provided. The Urban Institute identifies five types of
information that can be gathered (p.1):

(a)　　Constituents' satisfaction with the quality of specific
　　　services including identification of problem areas;

(b)　　facts such as the numbers and characteristics of users
　　　and nonusers of various services;

(c)   the reasons that specific services are disliked or
       not used;

(d)   potential demands for new services; and

(e)   citizen opinions on various community issues, including
       feelings of alienation towards Government and officials.

The information provided by such surveys can be very useful
in setting priorities for resource allocation and the
determination of actions to improve existing programmes.
In order for surveys to produce a valid view sample
sizes should be statistically reliable and those collecting
the information should be properly trained. Surveys are
costly because the in-person interview is generally
believed to be the most accurate form of survey. One
way of minimizing costs, currently used in the United
States, is the telephone survey. The Urban Institute
estimate the costs of an in-person interview at about
$15 (e.g., $11,250 for a survey of 750 respondents) when
external staff are employed. The cheapest form of survey
is by post, but generally there is a poor response.

In many instances the auditor may well decide that a citizen
survey is the only practical way to obtain feedback on the
quality of a particular service. The most cost-effective
approach would be to liaise with the programme management,

as the information is equally of use to them, and try and

jointly seek assistance from local college students (or some

similar body), on a part-time basis, who would be sufficiently

versed in statistical techniques and therefore require the

minimum of training.

Regression Analysis

New concepts in auditing require new auditing techniques.

In addition to the possible introduction of citizen surveys

the auditor should also consider the wider adoption of

mathematical techniques such as regression analysis.

Expressed in its simplest terms, regression analysis involves

selecting the effect of one or more performance indicators

(or independent variables) to the programme result (termed

the dependent variable). Simple regression analysis requires

some mathematical expertise but this should not be beyond

the competence of the auditor. At the very least he should

be able to recognize the potential application of regression

analysis and have access to specialists who can develop

proper computer packages.

Consider the situation where an auditor is asked to review

the effectiveness of a government programme designed to

improve the employment prospects of physically handicapped

people in selected types of industry. Whilst employment
statistics might be available showing the number of
handicapped people employed in these selected industries
this would not be a sufficient indicator of the programme's
success. One possible approach would be to select independent
variables that might have a direct or indirect effect on
the employment prospects of this group.

Such independent variables might include statistics on the
level of unemployed in the industry as a whole (distinguishing
between non-handicapped, physically handicapped and those
with other infirmities); demographic distribution of firms
in relation to specialist training centres; income levels
and so on. Once these results were derived from a multiple
regression model the auditor could then compare them with
results obtained with a non-control group. That is, compare
the results obtained with the results within industries not
covered by the programme. In this type of situation
regression analysis would be a valuable tool for the auditor,
providing him with information that would properly identify
the cause or causes that inhibit a programme from satisfactorily
achieving its objectives.

Factors Inhibiting The Introduction Of Effectiveness Auditing

Three factors are likely to inhibit the wider introduction

of VFM auditing in Britain and in particular, that component

that relates to effectiveness auditing. They are: (i) a

lack of political will; (ii) a lack of clearly defined

objectives; and (iii) the technical competence of the

audit staff. The first of these factors is outside the

influence of the auditor, other than by demonstrating the

value of his work in those limited areas where VFM auditing

is currently operating (though most of this work tends to

concentrate upon the economy and efficiency elements).

Problems of defining the objectives of a programme have

already been discussed earlier in relation to possible

conflicts that can arise between programme management

and the auditor. The prime reason for such disagreements

is usually because Parliament and Government fail to

express clearly programme objectives. Given this situation,

the auditor should endeavour to encourage departments

and agencies to review objectives, as they interpret

them, and hence formulate operational goals. (Such

goals were earlier defined as the aims and outcomes that

a programme purports to pursue and for which it can be

held accountable). It would then be up to Parliament or

Government to comment on these interpretations of objectives

and make such changes as they deemed necessary. This

would be an important role for the auditor since, being

impartial, he can cause both Government and Parliament,
on the one hand, and departments and agencies, on the
other, to be clear as to their common interests and
purpose. The auditor can contribute his experience, and
that of his specialist non-accountants, on how best to
formulate goals. He should also recommend that, if
necessary, management seek the views of independent
specialists. The success of the auditor in this field
will depend upon the trust that he can build up with
management.

The third factor relates to the technical competence of the
auditor and the staff that he directs; recall the words
of the Adams Report, quoted in Chaper 1. The role of the
auditor is constantly evolving and he is increasingly being
seen as a third party intermediary between Parliament,
Government, management and the public at large. Each
programme that the auditor investigates will in many respects,
be unique. The conduct of an effectiveness review does
not involve routine repetitive tasks. The issues addressed
and the approaches used may differ from study to study.
The auditor must be seen to be independent, impartial and
skilled. The 'Guide On The Program Evaluation Function',
produced by the Office of The Auditor General of Canada,
states (p.54):

"The independence of the evaluations is essential to the
production of objective and credible evaluation work. But
independence is not simply achieved by organisational
separation, although this is usually a prerequisite.
Independence also requires evaluators to be able to stand
back from the everyday concerns of a program's operation
and to look at what is going on in a detached, but not
uninformed, way. The evaluator must be able to identify,
articulate and question program assumptions at several
levels. The evaluator should not let personal biases
influence his or her view, and yet should be aware of the
environment and constraints under which the program operates.
While the evaluator may be convinced of the validity of
certain evidence or conclusions, he or she must remember
that the evaluator's task is to systematically (i.e. not
relatively) collect evidence to inform others. The
evaluation must be able to separate argument from evidence.
Conclusions must be based on evidence which others will
have to accept, including those who may not like the findings
produced. By being constantly conscious of the need for
independence, evaluators will enhance their own credibility
and the credibility of the findings."

In order for the auditor to enhance his knowledge of the

subject matter under investigation he may need to receive

assistance from specialists. This will be from three

sources:

(a)   Seconded by the programme management to provide

      guidance on problems of implementation. For example,

      a social services department might second two social

      workers to assist the auditor build up a picture of

      the workload and practices undertaken.

(b)   From external specialists. For example, if the auditor

was called upon to review the operations of a regional
airport he might well enlist the specialist knowledge
that a transport economist could provide;   particularly
with respect to externalities that could affect the
performance of the airport.

(c)   Specialist accounting and non-accounting staff who
      would work as full-time or part-time members of the
      audit team.

The composition of this third group will very much depend
upon the nature of the work undertaken by the auditor.   In
light of the present VFM exercises carried out in Britain
one might expect to find therein computer systems analysts,
educationalists, engineers, sociologists, and statisticians.

Academic accountants specializing in the problems of
Government and non-profit organizations also have an
important role to play by offering advice and education to
the profession.   Britain undertakes far less research into
public sector accounting problems than does the United
States, much of the rest of the EEC and prominent members
of the Commonwealth, in particular Australia, Canada and
New Zealand.

A Comprehensive Approach

Though time has been spent, in this chapter, discussing the
effectiveness element of a VFM audit, all three elements
are very much interrelated.   Indeed VFM auditing is often
referred to in the literature as Comprehensive Auditing.
Whilst it is true that there is little point to a programme
that, though efficient, fails to meet its stated operational
goals, it is equally true that effective programmes cannot
be undertaken regardless of cost.   Comprehensive auditing
as envisaged by the office of the Auditor General of Canada,
involves the reviewing and testing of financial systems and
internal controls - the financial audit - as well as
determining whether management has established systems and
procedures to ensure achievement of value for money.
Those VFM audits currently carried out in Local Government
and the Health Service are part of the overall audit brief
which also includes the more traditional financial audit.

In 'An Approach to Comprehensive Auditing' three
characteristics of comprehensive auditing are identified
by the Office of the Auditor General of Canada in order to
help to differentiate it from traditional auditing (p.5):

"In addition to being comprehensive, this audit approach
is co-ordinated, cyclical and constructive.

Co-ordination means co-ordination with and reliance on internal auditing to the maximum extent possible. The degree of reliance depends upon the extent and quality of internal comprehensive auditing, which can be one of the most effective tools available to management. As well, the various audit projects comprising the comprehensive audit are co-ordinated with one another, from the initial planning stages through to considering the impact of audit results in one project on other projects. Through greater co-ordination of auditing activities direct audit costs can be reduced as well as the indirect cost of disruption within the audited organization.

Cyclical means reporting on audit examinations at annual or longer intervals, where appropriate, depending upon the size, complexity and form of reporting of the organization. For example, the intent of the office is to be able to report on all major government entities at least once every five years. This results in more cost-effective audits, gives management time for reasonable corrective action and permits more thorough review by governing bodies such as Parliament, provincial legislatures, boards of directors and audit committees. Cyclical reporting does not necessarily mean that an entity will be audited only once every five years. In the case of the Office, work is done on a regular basis because:

- the Auditor General Act requirement for on opinion on the annual financial statements of the Government of Canada requires that certain auditing is carried out in all Government entities each year;

- significant matters rising from work done on an annual basis are regularly reported to Parliament; and

- follow up action taken by management on audit recommendations is an on-going process.

Constructive means that the auditor considers causes of weaknesses and suggests improvements to management, an important characteristic because of broader scope of issues being examined, evaluated and reported. Recommendations focus on 'what' needs improvement, not 'how to' do it, which of course is management's role. Reports to Parliament include mangement's responses to comprehensive audit recommendations."

This approach is very much along the lines that Parliament

should expect Government, at all levels, to adopt. It is

a process that reviews the accountability, in broad terms,

of all programmes which come under the ultimate control of

Government.

Case Study II: An Effectiveness Audit

This case study is based on an actual case reviewed by the

author.

The local authority involved wishes to remain anonymous.

A newly appointed Director of Social Services for a large

urban local authority, together with the Chief Executive

and Finance Officer, have asked the external auditor to

include a review of the authority's elderly day care centres

as part of his present VFM audit programme. They are

concerned that some £190,000 per annum is currently being

spent on running four centres with little idea of whether

the programme is effective in meeting the demand for this

facility within the community. The present level of operation

has grown over the last ten years but it is only in recent

years that notice has been taken of the expenditure involved.

All three officers expressed sympathy with the programme

but felt the need for an independent appraisal.

The authority has four centres. One centre (A) is adjacent

to a residential home and provides for residents and non-

residents alike. The facilities are available seven days

a week, from 9 a.m. to 9 p.m., and includes the provision

of lunch (at a nominal charge to non-residents). Recreational

facilities include a television lounge, newspapers and

periodicals, and board games. Supervision is provided by

a resident warden who also has a small full-time staff. A

variety of activities are also provided by local action

groups, such as concerts and day trips. The other three

centres (B, C and D) operate on a five-day-week basis

(from 10 a.m. to 4 p.m.) and are managed by a centre

supervisor who is expected to co-ordinate a range of

activities on a similar basis to that of centre A. These

three other centres have facilities (food etc.) provided

by the local authority but labour, other than that of the

supervisor, is provided free by voluntary workers.

The auditor initially thought that this investigation was

somewhat outside his abilities since he considered that it

was difficult to comment on the efficiency of the programme

(output measures not being pratical) and effectiveness

really meant 'as perceived by the reciepients of the service'.

Upon further consideration he decided upon an ad hoc approach
in two stages: first, to assess the demands and funds on
an individual centre basis and, second, to obtain the
assistance of an independent, university-based, sociologist
who had a special interest in the provision of community
services for the elderly.

Enquiries revealed that, as had been suspected, centre A
used the largest resources. It was considered to be the
best organized of the four centres with eighty residents
and sixty non-residents most days for lunch. In addition
it was estimated that upwards to three hundred other
elderly citizens used the centre on a casual basis. The
other three centres were very different. Centre B was a
large, but old, house which had poor facilities and
provided about twenty meals per day. The supervisor saw
her role as effectively that of only providing catering.

Centres C and D were both purpose built. Each attracted
about 60 people to lunch. Centre D also assisted in a
'meals on wheels' programme. In addition both centre
supervisors organized limited afternoon programmes for
these and a small number of other elderly citizens. It
was the auditor's judgement that, from a strictly financial
viewpoint, resources were well managed.

The sociologist suggested that each supervisor should be interviewed about their attitudes to the service they provided. In addition he proposed to survey selected recipients of the service as well as a sample of elderly citizens who, for one reason or another, chose not to use the facilities provided. The surveys were conducted by final-year sociology students.

The results revealed that the supervisor of centre A felt that, given the level of resources, a useful service was provided which was widely publicized in the community. There was also an active 'friends' committee which co-ordinated the contributions of the various action groups. The survey of recipients revealed that most were satisfied with the facilities. Suggestions were received for increased craft work facilities and these were passed on to the warden.

The results of the review of centre B were very unsatisfactory. Those who attended lunch did so only because it was convenient. The supervisor's views have already been outlined and these were matched by the views of elderly residents in the locality whose general attitude was that the centre's facilities and opening hours were singularly unattractive. Some of those interviewed wished that they could avail themselves of facilities at other centres but for a variety of reasons,

particularly transport difficulties, this had not been
possible.

The supervisors of centres C and D were rather disappointed
at the service they offered. The limited hours of opening
meant that they often had to turn down offers to perform
evening concerts and so on. Indeed, they felt that
facilities such as the television lounge should be available
until 9.30 p.m. Recipients also complained that insufficient
activities were provided and that the centres' opening
hours should be extended and also include some of the
weekend; for example, Saturday evenings and Sunday
afternoons. A significant proportion of the elderly
people in the survey who lived in the locality of either
centre, bud did not attend, stated that they agreed with
earlier comments and would use the centres if facilities
were improved.

In summary, the conclusions of the auditor and sociologist
were that:

1.   Resources at centre A were well applied and provided
      a welcome service to elderly citizens in the district.

2.   The facilities in centres B, C and D were under-
      utilized and did not provide a satisfactory level

of service.

3.   Centre B should be closed and that the released

operating funds be redeployed to centres C and D.

This would cover the costs of extended opening.

This in turn would enable these two centre supervisors

to organize a more attractive programme of activities

to satisfy those presently served and also attract

prospective users.

4.   Those who currently took meals at centre B should be

offered the services of the 'meals on wheels' programme

as the cost effect was considered minimal. In addition

it was suggested that the local authority might agree

to pay a petrol subsidy to volunteer drivers who could

take those adjacent to centre B to centre C to use

the (proposed) enhanced facilities.

5.   The authority should also have at its disposal the

site of centre B which could prove an attractive small

development. This opportunity was not costed other

than to ask the District Valuer to assess its value

if sold for redevelopment.

As a result of this review no funds were saved but it was

suggested that they be redistributed to provide a more
effective service that would also serve the needs of a
larger group of people.

The points to note from this case study are as follows:

(a)   As there had been no monitoring of this programme by
      management an ad hoc approach had to be adopted.
      (Management should now continue to monitor this
      programme's future operations.)

(b)   A non-accounting specialist was also involved who could
      independently assess the quality and effectiveness
      of the programme.

(c)   This particular example was deliberately structured
      so as to only consider the effectiveness aspect of
      a VFM audit.   It would be more normal to combine all
      three elements of VFM audit and more composite examples
      could be found at both local and central government
      levels.

Notes

1. There is a vast literature on budeting techniques for
    public sector and other not-for-profit organizations:
    see for example: Brown, R.L., Beyond Zero-base Budgeting,
    The Journal of Accounting, March 1981, pp.44-48, 50,
    52. Wildavsky, A., The Political Economy of Efficiency:
    Cost-Benefit Analysis, Systems Analysis, and Program
    Budgeting, Public Administration Review, December 1966,
    pp.292-310. Wildavsky, A., A Budget For All Seasons?
    Why The Traditional Budget Lasts, Public Administration
    Review, November/December, 1978, pp.501-509.

2. Adapted from p.14 of a paper presented by G.R. Berggren,
    Auditor General of Sweden, 'Effectiveness Auditing
    in Sweden's Central Government', 1980.

3. Taken from p.3 'Performance Measurement Manual and
    Catalogue', City of Thunder Bay. Original source:
    Lawton, P.J. and MacDonald, V.N., 'Improving Management
    Performance: The Contributions of Productivity and
    Performance Measurement", 1979.

4
Organizing A VFM Unit

The wider introduction of VFM audits is, as previously stated,
designed to expand the more traditional role of the auditor
- one limited to an examination of the accounting and
information systems. The question arises as to whether
VFM and traditional audits should be treated as distinct,
though complementary, or integrated into one comprehensive
audit. The former approach has been tried by both government
audit departments and private sector audit firms who undertake
audit work for public sector organizations. In Australia,
the Commonwealth Auditor General's department had a separate
VFM division. At the time of writing this division is
being phased out and its members integrated into the main
audit groups of the department. Private sector firms have
tended to use their consultancy divisions for many VFM
investigations and left the statutory audit work with
their audit practice. Even when a special division has
been created, for example to handle local authority audits,
the practice has been to second management consultants to

handle much of the VFM work. Such divisions are not

desirable in the long-term and can lead to a wide variety

of complications.

The creation of so-called specialist groups or sub-groups,

whilst acceptable on a short term basis as a means of

pooling scarce talent, can lead to an adverse effect on

the staff morale of those not engaged in VFM work. Those

who undertake the VFM audit aspects can sometimes be

observed to regard themselves as superior to their colleagues.

This is a mistaken notion since a sound financial audit is

a prerequisite to undertaking a VFM audit. By having two

distinct and separate groups of auditors there is often a

failure to cross-relate information and findings to maximum

effect. Equally, confusion is caused to the client's

staff who wonder at having to deal with two sets of auditors.

A more favoured approach is that adopted by the office of

the Canadian Auditor General whose comprehensive approach

to auditing is encompassed in the acronym FRAME (previously

referred to in Chapter 1). Its publication 'An Approach

To Comprehensive Auditing' (p.5) states:

"The scope of comprehensive auditing includes attesting to
financial and performance information related to accountability,
and satisfying any other specific requirements of the
mandate. The scope is also broad enough to permit a review

and report on the management of financial, human and
physical resources. This includes reviewing key management
activities and assessing the adequacy of related systems
and controls to ensure due regard for economy, efficiency
and effectiveness. One way of summarizing the scope is:
How do you know how well you are managing and how do you
report on (account for) that?"

The emphasis of this approach is to look behind the

statutory financial and stewardship requirements of

management to examine their internal systems and controls

for supporting the key activities of the particular

programmes that are selected for review. As will be

discussed further in Chapter 6, an integrated approach

meets more closely the wider demands that the audit

profession evolve and fulfil an expanded role both in

the government and private sectors. Further quotations

from this report emphasize this Canadian approach:

(p.7) "If the function of auditing is to add credibility
to reports, it is clear that the auditors' work itself
should be credible. Traditional auditing can look to
generally accepted auditing standards as bases for
establishing its credibility. In the case of comprehensive
auditing, both 'generally accepted management practices'
and the auditing standards needed to audit such practices
are still being determined and developed."

(p.8) "In areas where (audit) criteria do not already
exist, they can be derived from many sources including
pronouncements of professional organizations, government
regulations, directives, literature on the subject matter
being audited, respected professionals who work in the
area, and common sense, that is, what a reasonable person
would expect of management under the circumstances."

(pp.8-9) "Specialists in areas other than accounting and

auditing generally require some minimum training in auditing,
such as in using audit programs, gathering and documenting
evidence, conducting audit interviews, and so on. Accounting
and auditing specialists are taught comprehensive auditing,
but not necessarily up to the specialist level in the areas
of economy, efficiency and effectiveness. It is probably
more economical to recruit specialists in the value-for-
money areas, teach them the basics of comprehensive auditing
and then pair them with auditors. In this way they each
benefit from the other's perspective and experience."

It is certainly true that with the, as yet, limited

introduction of VFM auditing into the British public sector,

audit criteria need to be developed. Initial approaches

may have to be changed fairly often in an effort to gauge

their reasonableness, practicability and relevance. The

need to deploy non-accounting/audit specialists has previously

been referred to. At this stage it may only be economical

to employ such specialists on a part-time or consultancy

basis. Training is clearly all important and this should

be provided in the classroom on the job with the use of

'Audit Guides', and in multi-disciplinary postaudit reviews

on the performance and difficulties encountered by the

various members of the audit team.

An Overview Of the VFM Audit Process

The first stage in any audit is for both auditor and client

to agree on the terms of the engagement. Whilst legislation

and/or ministerial direction will dictate the general
requirements for the financial/regulatory phase of a
comprehensive audit, the same cannot be said of the VFM
audit. This is because it will only ever be possible to
examine a few select programmes in any amount of detail.
Legislation can only direct that VFM investigations
should take place and provide the auditor with the necessary
powers to undertake such tasks. It is for the auditor
ultimately to decide upon which areas he should investigate.

He should also expect the support of his professional
institute which should produce VFM audit guidelines and
standards that match the standard of those currently
produced for the traditional financial/regulatory audit.

Five stages in accepting a VFM audit engagement are set out
in a US publication, 'Operational Audit Engagements' (p.5):

". Identify the purpose(s) of the engagement (assessing
  performance, identifying opportunities for improvement,
  developing recommendations for improvement or further
  action, or some combination thereof) and the specific
  benefits expected to be obtained and consider their
  achievability.

 . Consider whether the scope of the engagement is sufficient
  to permit a substantive review of the function or activity
  being examined.

 . Determine whether the individual or entity requesting
  the service has the authority to do so.

• Consider whether the individuals assigned to perform the engagement possess competence in the technical subject matter under consideration.

• Reach an agreement with the engaging party about the nature and the scope of the work to be performed, the approach to be followed, and the nature of engagement reports. This agreement or undertaking is usually in writing, in the form of a proposal, contract or letter."

This final point is clearly important, indeed the phrase,

"usually in writing" would better read, "should be in

writing". Any written proposal should stress the following

aspects:[1]

(a)   purpose of the VFM investigation(s);

(b)   brief background of the engagement;

(c)   scope of the review: – areas/activities included
                                or excluded;

                               – sources and possible limitations
                                 of relevant data;

                               – other anticipated limitations;

(d)   approach and work plan to be followed;

(e)   evaluation criteria (established by management) to
       be reviewed;

(f)   course of action to be followed in the absence of
       such criteria (established by mangement) to be
       reviewed;

(g)   nature of end-products to be expected from the VFM
       audit particularly with respect to whether, and to
       what extent, recommendations for corrective actions
       are to be included;

(h)   staffing, including information about the use of
       outside specialists and the scope of their work;

(i)   extent of client involvement;

(j)   progress reports and meeting.

Once the terms of engagement have been agreed the general
sequence of activities involves making a brief audit survey
in order to plan the audit work; performing a field study;
analyzing the data collected; and preparing the final report.
Each of these phases is now discussed in turn.

(a) Survey and Plan.

The purpose of an initial survey is to orient the auditor
as to the various activities that are carried out within
a particular programme. Common questions that the auditor
might ask are provided by the Association of Government
Accountants in their monograph on 'Operational Auditing'
(p.21):

"What does the organization do?
 Where does it get its authority to do its work?
 Where does it get its money and how much does it get?
 Who runs the organization?
 What are its principal goals?
 What are its major problems?"

In obtaining answers to these questions the auditor will
build up a file of background material which should contain,
inter alia, applicable legislation and regulations;
organizational charts; policy statements, performance

standards; and past performance data. Additionally, the
auditor should also arrange meetings with senior personnel,
such as the programme director, councillors (if a local
authority assignment), etc. In the field of health
care, for example, the auditor would wish to address
both members and management of the Health District (or
Region) in which the investigation is to be carried out.
It is important that there should be an understanding of
the purpose(s) of the VFM assignment and an early discussion,
at senior level, of the expected benefits that might be
expected.

This preliminary stage should acquaint the auditor with an
understanding of the issues that concern management, issues
raised in previous investigations and an idea of potential
areas of uneconomical or inefficient operation. The final
step in the survey stage is the preparation of a detailed
audit plan which should be a detailed version of the outline
work plan included in the engagement documentation. Such
a plan should: define the overall approach or scope to the
investigation; indicate those matters that may require
particular attention; and identify and then allocate
resource requirements. Those areas that may require particular
attention will generally be those that from an initial
review by the auditor indicate that costs can be reduced

or programme results can be improved.

Any VFM audit plan is unlikely to be as detailed as that

for a financial audit. Whereas the latter may stipulate

the use of clear cut audit procedures which must be done,

such as verifying accounts receivable, checking inventory

balances and reconciling cash, the same uniform approach

is not true of a VFM audit plan. The view of the Association

of Government Accountants is that the audit plan (or

programme) should be evolutionary (p.39):

"One difficulty in doing operational (or in our terminology
VFM) audits is that the condition uncovered by the detailed
audit work often does not turn out to be quite the same as
was initially anticipated. Development of a finding is
frequently an evolutionary process in actual practice.
Thus the audit program should also be designed to be
evolutionary. The audit program should show:

What is known for sure, i.e. any components of the findings
that have been fully developed.
What is suspected but needs more work to substantiate.
Areas needing full development.

The audit plan should be updated periodically as work
progresses.... When plans are revised, it is highly
recommended that audit program changes be reduced to writing
along with the appropriate reasons whenever such plans are
revised.
Experience has shown that important information is overlooked
when changes in audit direction and scope are not written
in the audit program."

When deciding what evaluation criteria are to be examined

or developed, the audit plan should distinguish clearly those used for measuring efficiency from those used in reviewing

effectiveness.

(b)   Field Study.

Following the initial survey and planning stage there should

be a fairly detailed field study. Key personnel at all

organizational levels should be interviewed. For example,

suppose that the operations of a Passenger Transport Authority

were under investigation. Appropriate people would include

the Transport Committee Chairman (probably a local authority

councillor), the chief executive officer and various

departmental managers on aspects of administration and

service provision. More junior grades of management would

also be interviewed. A bus inspector would be well qualified

to give a first hand account of operational matters such

as adherence to timetables, under-utilized services etc.

If the nature of the programme permits, external interviews

should also take place. To continue this example, it

might be useful to survey passengers on various aspects of

the service presently provided.

Other aspects of the field study would include observation

of various operational activities, including work flow.

Data would be collected on demand for services and workloads undertaken. If efficiency measures were in use these would

be examined, otherwise ad hoc measures would, if practicable,

have to be devised. Similarly the auditor would have to

satisfy himself that programmes were in accordance with pre-

determined objectives (i.e. determine that programmes were

not just efficient but also effective).

There are, therefore, three aspects to the field study

planned by the auditor; it helps him:[2]

(i)   understand programme objectives and the objectives
       stated by programme managers;

(ii)   determine the extent to which objectives are measurable;
       and

(iii) determine whether he is in agreement with the audited
       organization on the relationship between programme
       objectives as specified by management.

It is, in effect, an examination of the key management

activities, systems and controls that are critical for the

efficient and effective operations of the programme.

(c)   Analyzing the Data.

As a result of field work the auditor should be in a

position to analyze all the data that he has collected.

This will be in four principal categories: physical,

testimonial, documentary and analytical.[3]

"1. Physical evidence is the type an auditor obtains by direct observation of what people are doing, the condition of property or of similar matters. The auditor becomes, in essence, a witness to the problem he is researching when he examines the physical evidence.
2. Testimonial evidence is gathering data from those who have witnessed a situation or event which the auditor was unable to observe. The auditor should prepare a written record of the pertinent information obtained in such interviews, for support of his findings included in his report.
3. Documentary evidence is what the auditor obtains by the examination of the documents pertaining to the matter under audit.
4. Analytical evidence is evidence which the auditor proposes by putting together data he has gathered to create new information or to use in a presentation to management of the organization."

As the auditor formulates his findings he should discuss them with management. His conclusions will not just be based on whether greater economies can be obtained. It may be that changes could improve efficiency, redeploy expenditure to provide a more effective service, or lead to improved information to enable management to monitor the future development of the programme.

(d) The Final Report.

Reporting is the final phase of the audit process. Such reports are much longer than the brief certification provided under a financial audit. The Association of Government Accountants regards every VFM audit as having certain common structural characteristics which can be regarded as the building blocks from which a fully developed audit

finding is made. Their monograph on 'Operational Auditing'

(p.5) states:

"The audit can use these building blocks to construct a
finding that will provide the organization audited or
other readers with all the information needed and the
reason for his recommendations. The building blocks are...:

Authority - general authority to conduct the activity under
audit.
Goal - what the activity under audit is or should be trying
to achieve.
Policy - the general guidance given by management on how
to achieve the goal.
Condition - extent to which goals are being achieved.
Effect - beneficial results from achieving goals or if goals
are not being achieved, the loss in pounds or in effectiveness
caused by failing to meet goals.
Procedures or Practices - ways of doing things that have
been established to guide employees toward attainment of
the prescribed policies and goals.
Cause - reasons why procedures or practices were effective
if goals are being achieved or the reasons why they were
not effective if goals are not being achieved.
Conclusion - argument for a change in policy or in procedure
or practice to bring about achievement of desired goals.
If goals are being achieved, the conclusion will doubtless
be not to change.
Recommendation - steps that should be taken to make the
changes needed to achieve desired goals. The building
blocks are arranged in the order in which they generally
should be presented to an uninformed reader to enable him
to assimilate the information in a sequence that will be
meaningful to him. This is not necessarily the order in
which the auditor will obtain the information during the
audit.

(Note: These characteristics are usually included only when
the auditor finds that goals are not being achieved. If
he finds that goals are being achieved, these characteristics
are usually omitted from his report although they may be
included to show precisely what procedures or practices are
effective and why they were effective.)"

Draft reports should be discussed with management as their
views might usefully be incorporated into the final report.
For example, management may well agree that certain criticisms
are justified but wish it stated, in their defence, that
the prime cause is due to ambiguous legislation or lack of
precise policy statements at a higher level. Alternatively,
the auditor may wish to record the dissenting views of
management when there is a lack of agreement on the
recommendations proposed. When external specialists are
employed it may also be useful to present their findings
as an appendix to a shorter form of report.

No guidance can be offered as to the length of the report.
This really depends on the initial findings of the
investigation and the skill of the auditor in presenting
his information. Good writing is hard work. Technical
jargon should be avoided as far as possible, and the auditor
should bear in mind that his report will be read by a
variety of people.

Amongst those interested in the report and its findings may
be the client, management, unions, politicians and the
public (either individually or represented by organizations
such as pressure groups, consumer councils etc.).

In the final analysis, having considered all the available
data, the auditor must exercise his judgement: judgement
as to the conclusions and recommendations he wishes to make,
supported by relevant information (in sufficient detail).

Relationship Between External And Internal Auditors

The duties performed by the internal auditor should be seen
to be complementary to the work performed by the external
auditor.   This applies for both financial and VFM audits.
The external auditor should review the work of the internal
audit staff to determine their effectiveness in assisting
management to improve the quality of information that is
necessary if they are satisfactorily to monitor the
efficiency and effectiveness of the programmes under their
charge.

Internal audit is an integral part of internal control.
The extent to which the external auditor can dispense with
detailed work depends in no small part on the effectiveness
of the system of internal control. This will be all the
more so with the wider introduction of VFM audits. However,
the standard of internal audit in the public sector is not
generally very good. It has been seen as a 'necessary evil'
for ensuring that the conduct of those responsible for

operating an organization remains within prescribed rules,

regulations and legislation. One would have hoped that

with the development in recent years of operational auditing

that departments and agencies would have up-graded their

internal audit function. Government should review the

present standard of internal audit within public sector

administration, especially at the central government level.

One must presently conclude that management does not view

the current internal audit function as a significant service

- thus questioning its very raison d'etre.

In other countries there has been a trend to expand the roles

of internal audit to meet part of the growing public concern

that the administration of government be subject to regular

review and control. For example, the Commonwealth Government

of Australia has, in recent years, devoted much attention

to the quality of service from its internal audit staff.

Criticisms contained in various Auditor-General's reports

could be just as easily directed at the British public sector.

They have noted in particular:[4]

". division of internal audit staff to other duties, reducing
   effectiveness of the internal audit function;
 . arrears of work resulting in inadequate coverage by
   internal audit;
 . audit methodology not geared to a system-based approach;
 . emphasis on error detection rather than on evaluating

the adequacy of control systems, resulting in fragmentation
and inadequate coverage of operations;
. working papers not providing adequate documentation on
the scope and quality of the audits in a manner necessary
for audit management; and
. inadequate knowlege of ADP for auditing effectively
computerized systems.

In 1977 the Commonwealth Public Service Board received an

Efficiency Review of Internal Audit conducted by a leading

firm of management consultants. They found that internal

audit arrangements were most unsatisfactory. The report

stated that in the Australian Public Service there were more

than six hundred staff employed in the internal audit

function and the total salary bill was over $7 million per

year. In terms of value for money, the report stated that

its authors were:

"...unable to identify sufficient tangible benefits arising
from the present internal audit effort which would justify
staffing and expenditure of this magnitude."

Since this report the Australian Public Service Board has

brought about a rapid improvement in the quality of internal

audit provided. (See Chapter 5.)

An effective internal audit function is needed to foster

high standards of management control practice. It follows,

therefore, that the external VFM auditor would be well

advised to evaluate the extent to which internal audit
staff are used in this area. This should be done at the
survey stage of the assignment.

The Role of a VFM Audit Committee

The origins of audit committees can be traced back to the
nineteenth century when the first limited liability companies
were audited by committees of shareholders on behalf of their
fellow equity investors. Such was the nature of affairs
then that investors, who were relatively few in number,
elected from amongst their number those more able to
safeguard the interests of the majority. Within a few
decades this task was passed over to firms of professional
auditors. Just as the auditing role was waived by
shareholders, so too was the day-to-day management of
these companies which passed to full-time managers who, as
executive directors, determine company policy and future
direction. Very often these directors have no, or at best
only a nominal, equity interest.

At present there exists in the private sector a debate,
which has parallels in the public sector, on the whole
nature of the relationship between shareholders, management
and auditors. This has arisen because over time there has

developed a 'divorce' of interest between management and
shareholders. Directors, whilst endeavouring to serve the
best interests of shareholders, also have responsibilities
to employees, suppliers, customers etc. (and perhaps their
own interests). A similar position also arose in Canada
and the United States where audit committees have been
re-established using non-executive external directors
whose role is to safeguard the long-term interests of
shareholders.

Audit committees were first publicly endorsed in the United
States in 1940 by both the Securities and Exchange Commission
(SEC) and the New York Stock Exchange (NYSE). Interest arose
following the deception of shareholders by four executive
directors (later found to be brothers); the case is now well
documented: McKesson and Robbins, 1939. Much later, in
1976 the NYSE introduced a requirement for audit committees
into its listing agreement. The SEC, in individual cases,
has required certain corporations to establish audit
committees with specific duties. In Canada, the Business
Corporation Act 1975, requires public corporations to have
an audit committee of not less than three directors. Here
in Britain, it has long been argued that similar committees
should be (re)introduced. Whilst shareholders legally
appoint the auditor, they have no automatic right of

communication, other than receiving his report. In the

words of de Paula and Attwood (p.341):

"An audit committee of outside directors, with shareholders'
interests in the forefront of their minds, can have
effective communication with the auditor to discuss and
probe the detailed matters which are of concern to
shareholders, and which the shareholders might have
themselves wished to discuss with the auditor were they
permitted to do so."

The Auditing Practices Committee (APC) of the Consultative

Committee of Accountancy Bodies (CCAB) commissioned Richard

Buckley to write a report, published in 1979, on the role

of audit committees. He stated that audit committees can:

"(a) help directors to fulfil their responsibilities;
 (b) strengthen the role of non-executive directors;
 (c) strengthen the objectivity and credibility of financial
     reporting;
 (d) strengthen the independence of the audit function;
 (e) improve the quality of the audit and accounting
     functions;
 (f) improve communications between directors, auditors,
     and management."

Such committees therefore assist shareholders, as owners

of the company, in ensuring that management are seen to be

accountable.

The parallels in recommending the establishment of audit

committees is to offer one remedy for bridging the gap that

has arisen between Parliament, Government bureaucracy and

the public at large. As will be explained in Chapter 6,

one of the greatest dangers with the introduction of VFM

auditing is that its success may well flounder because basic

questions of principle, concerning the very nature of

accountability in the public sector, have yet to be addressed.

Audit committees could well be introduced at all levels of

the public sector; for example, at Local Government and

Regional Health Authority levels, as well as within certain

sectors of central government. Whilst local authorities

have elected councillors and regional health authorities

appointed by the Secretary of State for Health and Social

Services, they are very much involved in current management

problems and short-term planning. They are heavily

influenced by the advice that they receive from senior

public servants who, as with their private sector executive

director counterparts, must have regard to competing

interests.

A mechanism would need to be found to appoint such committees.

They should clearly be independent of the day-to-day

management of the organization. Committees should be

small and composed of 'informed' people. For example,

members of a local authority auditing committee might be

drawn from the local chamber of commerce, rate-payers

association etc. The purpose being to appoint public

interest, non-political members. It would also be very

necessary to define clearly their responsibilities and

duties. As might be expected members of these audit

committees would be more interested in VFM aspects of the

audit report than the purely financial aspects.

Buckley's advantages could be restated such that the

advantages of establishing a VFM audit committee would be

to:

(a)   help elected/appointed individuals and public servants
       fulfil their responsibilities;

(b)   strengthen the influence of the public at large;

(c)   strengthen the objectivity and credibility of both
       financial and VFM reporting;

(d)   strengthen the independence of the audit function;

(e)   improve the quality of the audit, accounting and
       management information systems;

(f)   improve communication between elected/appointed
       individuals, public servants and the public at large.

Audit committees would also need some form of recourse,

should they feel that their viewpoints were not fully

considered. Practically this could be to the respective

Secretary of State and, more ideally, also to the C&AG/PAC.

Notes

1.   Adapted from Operational Audit Engagements, p.8,
      General Accounting Office (USA), 1978.

2.   Adapted from An Approach To Comprehensive Auditing,
      p.30, Office of the Auditor General, Ottawa, September
      1981.

3.   Association of Government Accountants (USA),
      Operational Auditing, p.53, Monograph No. One, 1978.

4.   Connelly, D.M., 'Internal Audit - The Poor Relation
      of the Public Service', p.14, Australian Journal of
      Public Administration, Vol. XXXIX, No. 1, March 1980.

5
International Perspectives On VFM Auditing

VFM auditing is not new; in many ways Britain is only now
embarking, explicitly, upon a path that other countries have
already followed. This chapter reviews developments in five
countries. The first three are members of the British
Commonwealth - Canada, Australia and New Zealand. Each
country retains what might, loosely, be termed a 'Westminster'
style of government. Canada was the first to adopt VFM,
which together with regulatory audit requirements, is
called in their terminology 'Comprehensive Auditing'. In
Australia, the Federal Government has adopted Efficiency
Audits whilst individual states are currently re-appraising
their audit role. In the state of Victoria, for example,
much thought has been given to measuring the effectiveness
of departments and individual programmes.

The fourth country considered is the United States of
America, where the Comptroller General, as head of the
General Accounting Office (GAO), both formulates overall

accounting principles, standards and requirements and

conducts investigations and audits. The final country

considered is Sweden, since its National Audit Bureau was

the first in Europe to adopt formally VFM auditing in

1970.

Much of the material for this chapter has been supplied by

each country's national audit office. This material tends

to discuss mainly the philosophy and recommended techniques

for undertaking VFM audits. However, little documentary

evidence is available on what actually happens in practice.

Therefore, an important caveat is that there may be wide

divergencies between the recommended approaches and practice.

Canada

Until 1973, the staff of the Auditor General were primarily

engaged on transactions auditing. With the appointment of

the new Auditor General, James J. Macdonell, there was a

redefinition of the audit role into more contemporary terms.

An independent review committee was established to look at

the responsibilities of the Office; its relationship with

Government departments and agencies; its reporting procedures;

and the means by which the independence of the Office could

be assumed. As Macdonell stated (p.2):

"Did the Auditor General have the right to examine and
report on more than just the legality of expenditures?
For example, how far can he go in commenting on whether or
not they had been made with due regard to economy,
efficiency and effectiveness?"

The review committee, which consisted of two accountants
and a lawyer, tabled its report to parliament in 1975.

The most important recommendation of the Review Committee
was that the Auditor General should be concerned as to
whether value had been received for public money expended
and should report adverse findings to Parliament. This
recommendation was embodied in the Auditor General Act of
1977 which requires the Auditor General to report to the
House of Commons when:

"...money has been expended without due regard to economy
or efficiency, or satisfactory procedures have not been
established to measure and report the effectiveness of
programs, where such procedures could appropriately and
reasonably be implemented."

At the same time, under the Executive Interchange Program
of the Public Services Commission, the Financial Management
and Control Study (FMCS) was established. The services of
twenty partners and twenty senior employees of nineteen
national firms of chartered accountants were obtained.
This private sector input of professionals was matched by

a group of senior staff from the Auditor General's department.

The study was completed in twenty four months and the

results of the study were conveyed in the 1976 report of

the Auditor General to parliament when he stated that

"Parliament - and indeed the Government itself - has lost,

or is close to losing, effective control of the public

purse". In accepting the key recommendations of this

report, the Government appointed the first Comptroller

General of Canada and set up a Royal Commission on Financial

Management and Accountability which reported in 1979.

The 1977 Auditor General's Annual Report revealed that there

were serious weaknesses in the financial control and security

systems of the majority of Government computer installations.

In the 1978 Annual Report (the Centennial Report) the results

of the first VFM audits were disclosed. Thirty-five studies

were carried out in twenty-three departments. The Auditor

General reported (Macdonell, p.5):

"...there is, in my opinion, widespread lack of due regard
for economy and efficiency in the operations of the
Government, and inadequate attention to determining whether
programmes costing many millions of dollars are accomplishing
what Parliament intended.... A review of 23 programs in
18 departments has disclosed few successful attempts to
evaluate the effectiveness of programs."

Additionally this report had one hundred pages devoted to

the improvements that were required.

Independent of government measures, the Canadian Institute

of Chartered Accountants (CICA) established a special

committee, chaired by John W. Adams. The Adams report,

published in 1978, endorsed VFM audits as appropriate for

all levels of government; it stated that (p.42):

"In the not-for-profit area these incentives (i.e.
profitability, competitive environment) are absent and, as
a consequence, it may be appropriate to extend the audit
of such enterprises to encompass the economy, efficiency
and effectiveness of the enterprise's operations (the
'value-for-money' audit).

...We believe that this type of audit is appropriate for
all levels of government: provincial, regional and municipal.
In time it should be extended to cover public organizations
such as hospitals and universities, in addition to all of
the non-commercial Crown corporations. It may also be
appropriate in the audit of charities."

All of these moves, at federal level, provided the impetus

that has led to the present 'comprehensive' approach to

auditing, with its key element of VFM auditing. Provinces

now also have legislation similar to that for the Auditor

General of Canada. Both Ontario and British Columbia

reported under expanded mandates in 1979. As Macdonell

stated (p.6):

"The research and the hundreds of recommendations flowing
from these... studies produced a substantial body of
knowledge and a methodology which forms the basis of a new

approach to public sector auditing. This approach is
designed to assure taxpayers that Governments are spending
public money with due regard to economy, efficiency and
effectiveness. We call it comprehensive auditing".

The Office of the Auditor General of Canada defines

comprehensive auditing as follows (An Approach to

Comprehensive Auditing, p.1):

"'Comprehensive auditing' is the term used by the Office
of the Auditor General and others to describe the broad-
based auditing approach which is aimed at systematically
reviewing and reporting on accountability relationships
and on the supporting activities, systems and controls
employed by management in fulfilling its responsibilities.'

This definition confers upon the auditor a very wide mandate

which has two central themes: accountability and value-for-

money. Figure 3 was originally presented in the 'Report

of the Independent Committee for the Review of the Office

of the Auditor General of Canada'. It defines the terms

accountability and audit, adopted by the Committee as most

appropriate, and depicts the relationship between Parliament,

Government and the Auditor General. The definition of

accountability stresses the importance of reporting upon

the manner in which duties have been discharged. This

means reporting upon the way that tasks were performed,

indicating why a particular strategy(strategies) was adopted

and providing an analysis of the results achieved. It is

Figure 3

Accountability

. . . the obligation to answer for a responsibility that has been conferred. It presumes the existence of at least two parties: one who allocated the responsibility and one who accepts it with the undertaking to report upon the manner in which it has been discharged.

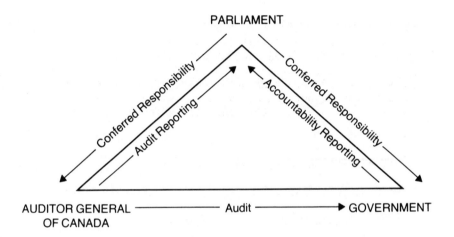

Audit

. . . a process that is super-imposed on an accountability relationship. It is carried out to establish that a report on the responsibility assumed is a correct and fair one. An audit is usually performed by a third party, primarily serving the interests of the party who delegated the responsibility.

(Source: Report of the Independent Committee for the Review of the Office
of the Auditor General of Canada. Ottowa: Information Canada,
1975, p.9.)

not thought acceptable to report simply that $x millions
of appropriated funds were spent on a particular programme.
The audit reviews whether management have discharged their
responsibilities Whilst the auditor is primarily responsible
to parliament he clearly can also provide valuable
information to management. The Office of the Auditor
General of Canada has developed an acronym FRAME which
identifies and explains the components of a Comprehensive
Audit (previously outlined in Chapter 1). This role is
directed toward the accountability of Government to
Parliament for the administration of public programmes,
that is, the administrative side of Government rather than
the policy-making, political side. While this distinction
might appear clear it is in fact often difficult for the
auditor not to comment on policy.

The legislated authority for comprehensive auditing is
contained in Section 7 of the Auditor General Act. The
form of reporting is the annual Auditor General's Report
to the House of Commons. This report includes chapters
dealing with:

(a)   results of comprehensive audits within Government
       department and agencies;

(b)   results of Government-wide studies;

(c)   other significant matters, such as those arising

out of audit work carried out in departments and
agencies in non-comprehensive audit reporting years;

(d)   follow-up on previously reported matters; and

(e)   certain qualifications and other matters included in
       audit reports on the financial statements of agencies
       and crown corporations.

The Auditor General of Canada examines the affairs of

departments of the Government of Canada and of federally

funded entities. At the second level of Government in the

provinces, there is also an Auditor General, e.g. the

Ontario (Canada) Provincial Auditor. His sphere of auditing

is the provincial departments and entities which receive

funding from that level of Government. Each province also

has requirements for periodic independent audits of local

Government. There appear to be significant differences in

the accounting principles adhered to by municipal entities

but there are no specific provisions for performance audits.

Australia

The Auditor General for the Commonwealth of Australia is

appointed under the Audit Act 1901 - the fourth Act of the

Parliament to receive assent. Amendments to the Act in 1979

gave the Auditor General the power to accept appointments

as auditor of government non-departmental bodies and to conduct efficiency audits of departments and other government

bodies. Further, whenever legislation establishes

Commonwealth statutory authorities, the Auditor General is

invariably designated as auditor. The present Deputy

Auditor General, D.J. Hill, expresses the objectives of

the Auditor General's office as (p.417):

"...to audit the various operations and undertakings of
Government so as to form opinions on Government administration
and report on those opinions to the Parliament; and

...to present independent and objective reports directed
to stimulating improvements in public administration".

The 1979 Act was primarily motivated by the recommendations

of the Royal Commission on Australian Government Administration

which reported in 1976.

The amended Act was concerned with the efficiency and

economy in the use of resources with which an organization

achieves its defined operational objectives. A review of

effectiveness is not part of the Auditor General's mandate.

That role has been given to the Department of the Prime

Minister and Cabinet. The efficiency audits reported upon

to date have been undertaken as discrete projects separate

from any other audit coverage of the organization and have

been substantially carried out by staff of the Efficiency

Audit Division. Currently this division is being phased

into the other audit divisions to promote the multi-

disciplinary approach that already exists in Canada and

the United States.

Until recently, efficiency audit reports have been published

separately, being fairly substantial documents. The most

recent efficiency report, at the time of writing, was

included towards the end of the May 1983 Report of the

Auditor General. It was concerned with the management of

the main battle tank by the Department of Defence capital

outlay of approximately $150 million and direct operating

costs of $14 million per annum. It was only nine pages in

length. Whilst most commentators would concur with a

multi-disciplinary approach to VFM audits and the need for

more reporting by exception when VFM audits and regulatory

audits are combined, there must be some cause for concern

that one reason attributed to this change was political

pressure from successive Governments who were resentful of

one or two earlier reports. It does seem sensible, however,

to move towards a more integrated approach since this

should lead to a greater sharing of information and exchange

of ideas amongst audit staff.

As stated above, the Auditor General has no effectiveness

review function; this is within the purview of the

Department of the Prime Minister and Cabinet and the

conclusions of such reviews (if they be carried out) are

not published. No state Government in Australia has given

an effectiveness review function to an Auditor General.

New South Wales, in line with the Commonwealth, has given

the Premier's Department this function. The State of

Victoria is currently re-assessing the scope and

responsibilities of its Auditor General. All present

indications are that forthcoming legislation will grant

him the authority to undertake effectiveness reviews. As

a recent Victorian discussion paper, Review of the Audit

Act 1958, stated (p.37):

"...efficiency and effectiveness are not really different
concepts, but are concerned with evaluation at different
levels of management with differing levels of
responsibilities. It also follows that it is quite possible
for an organization to efficiently carry out ineffective
tasks."

This quotation was prefaced by an example which could be

usefully repeated: consider a project to construct a new

by-pass. Efficiency in carrying out the prescribed task

of building the road would be represented by a cost per

mile, or something similar. But effectiveness would be

represented by the extent to which the by-pass achieved

its planned objectives of reducing travel time, reducing

accidents and reducing transport costs. In this illustration

one is really dealing with different levels of management.

In measuring efficiency (cost per mile) it is really the

performance of the project engineer that is being evaluated.

He is not responsible for the project achieving its

objectives. In measuring effectiveness one is evaluating

the decisions of those responsible for choosing the project,

i.e. top management. The view was taken that (p.9):

"Generally efficiency can be seen as measuring the
achievement of lower level management's objectives and
effectiveness with top management's objectives. This is
what is meant by the common statement that effectiveness
is concerned with policy issues and efficiency with issues
of administration. Efficiency measurement takes the policy
objectives as given."

Later the discussion paper listed the following arguments

in favour of effectiveness audits (p.39):

"...it may be argued that:

-       permanent heads have significant 'policy'
        responsibilities in terms of being responsible for
        many decisions concerning the choice of particular
        programmes or strategies, quite apart from their
        important role as policy advisers to ministers;

-       in any case it is quite appropriate for policy
        decisions made by ministers to be publicly reviewed;

-       such objectives do not necessarily involve questioning

Government objectives, only the methods chosen to achieve them; and

—   in determining its view on the effectiveness of Government programmes Parliament should use independent evaluations such as those of the Auditor General;

and therefore that effectiveness reviews could be undertaken by an Auditor General with powers to report to Parliament."

Whilst the Commonwealth Government may have taken the lead in expanding the role of the Auditor General, future developments in Victoria should endow its Auditor General with much wider powers of investigation.

At both Commonwealth and State levels, there has been some disagreement as to whether an efficiency audit function belongs with a Public Service Board rather than with the Auditor General's Office. To a large extent this disagreement has reflected a failure to appreciate the complementary roles of these two review organizations — the Auditor General providing independent reports to Parliament and the Public Service Board being (for this function) part of the executive branch of Government and reporting to the executive. An efficiency audit, perhaps more than effectiveness review, is a logical extension of the traditional financial and compliance audit. The external auditor already has an accepted role in commenting on cases of waste, extravagance or failures in financial control systems. The examination of internal control

systems is common to financial, compliance and efficiency

audits. This is explicitly recognized in Canadian

literature (the comprehensive auditing approach) and

implicitly recognized in Australian practice.

Attention has also been given, at Commonwealth level, to

enhancing the role of internal audit to include non-financial

matters. The Public Service Board has been responsible for

upgrading audit establishments and providing training in

audit methodology and computer auditing. In 1983, a Public

Service Board report stated (p.ii):

"Virtually all departments considered that they received
value for money from their internal audit services in 1982.
For the service as a whole only 4% of audit recommendations
were rejected. The major audit units reported reasonable
correlation in 1982 between their audit plans and audit
performance but some others were not completely satisfied
with the progress or standard achieved to date."

Although internal audit performance is not yet optimal there

have been farreaching improvements in recent years.

New Zealand

In New Zealand, the Public Finance Act 1977 provided for

an independent audit agency - the Audit Office. It consists

of the Auditor General, his Deputy, officers of the Audit

Department and any other persons whom the Auditor General

may appoint to carry out his functions. The independence

of the Auditor General is preserved by:

(a)   making him responsible only to Parliament (S.33);

(b)   preserving his department's freedom from Ministerial

       direction (S.15(5));

(c)   preventing the reduction of audit staff's salaries

       (S.18(2));

(d)   providing for dismissal only on certain grounds

       and then only by the Governor General on receipt

       of an address from Parliament (S.20),

(e)   authority to conduct VFM audits (S.25(3)).

Paragraph 102 of the Audit Department's internal manual

states:

"The emphasis throughout the statutory mandate is on the
Audit Office forming its opinion and communicating to
external parties. This is the essential vehicle by which
the Audit Office communicates its findings to the outside
world and forms its part in the accountability loop. The
professionalism, independence and objectivity of the opinion
and report is therefore crucial to the credibility, usefulness
and ultimate survival of the Office. The essential nature
of the environment in which the Audit Office exists means
that in communicating its findings to the outside world
heed has to be taken of the political implications, the
desire to achieve change within the administration being
audited, and preferability of constructive reporting rather
than on negative reporting of erroneous transactions and

wasteful events. The crux of the credibility of the
Office's reporting function therefore rests on the adoption
of a systems based approach to the audit function. The
systems based approach means that auditors should focus
in their reporting and field work on management systems
– the decision making, execution and control processes –
rather than on individual officers, transactions and events."

As in Canada, the New Zealand Audit Office has summarized

the concept of their audit function into an acronym – CARE:

C Control – the evaluation of management controls over the

  resources for which it is responsible.

A Attest and Authority – the expression of an opinion on

  financial statements and the verification of the authority

  for material and financial transactions.

R Reporting – to Parliament, ministers and other external

  parties on matters arising from audits.

E Effectiveness and Efficiency – the giving of an opinion

  on whether audited entities have applied their resources

  in an effective and efficient manner consistent with the

  policy of the governing body of that entity.

The CARE philosophy was initially introduced in 1975; it

is a comprehensive approach which comprises an annual

examination of financial statements together with an annual

examination of some _aspects_ of the organization, with a
view to giving an opinion on value for money and management
controls generally.

VFM audits are initiated when the auditor:

(a)   wishes to confirm initial suspicions on any deficiency
       in a management system; or

(b)   wishes to consider the internal controls in operation
       that purport to demonstrate the level of effectiveness
       and/or efficiency of expenditure programmes or resource
       use.

Paragraph 808 of the Audit Office manual discusses VFM audit
reports; it states:

"(a)   Reports should:

       (i)   disclose the policies under which the entity
              operates those activities which are subject to
              audit;

       (ii)   give an opinion as to whether (and to what
              degree) funds under the control of the entity
              are being administered in manner which is
              consistent with identified policies;

       (iii) give an opinion on the adequacy of systems (if
              any) in operation for assessing relative
              effectiveness and/or efficiency;

       (iv)   give an opinion if possible as to whether funds

under the control of the entity are being
considered in a manner which results in the
effective and/or efficient use of resources;

(v)   identify the areas where improvements in
organizational systems and procedures could
result in a more effective or efficient use of
resources;

(vi)   identify the areas where improvement in data
collection and reporting processes could lead
to better performance measures.

(b)   Reports should be at two levels:

(i)   a synopsis report to the elective body in such
a manner that information disclosed therein will
be publicly reported;

(ii)   a detailed report to appropriate levels of
management indicating the specific improvements
which could be made to administrative and
organizational systems, controls and procedures."

New Zealand's experience of VFM audits is relatively recent

and to date the Audit Office has carried out about forty

such audits. Present experience has shown that most

organizations have not yet developed (when considered

possible) some form of productivity measure whereby

efficiency could be monitored. As a consequence audit

staff have been able to give only general comments on how

efficiently an organization is run with particular emphasis

being reserved for when inefficiencies are apparent.

The Audit Office has often acknowledged the fact that it

cannot perform adequately in the VFM auditing area solely

with accounting based skills. Their experience has been

that, rather than bring into their audit groups non-accounting

based auditors, it is better for the traditional aspects

of auditing (i.e. the design of audit tests, the gathering

of evidence and the reporting thereon) to be done by staff

auditors with consultants to be used to advise in the

planning stages and to assist in the development of

meaningful reporting. Consultants have generally been

drawn, on secondment, from line management positions in

either the public sector or private sector.

United States Of America

In the USA the role of the General Accounting Office (GAO)

is somewhat incongruous since the basic principle of audit

independence is called into question. The GAO is headed

by the Comptroller General of the USA who is appointed for

a fixed term of fifteen years. The Comptroller and his

department perform a dual role. On the one hand, the GAO

formulates the overall principles, standards and requirements

for the accounting systems of individual federal agencies

and also the central accounting system of the Treasury

Department. This role is provided for under the provisions

of the Budget and Accounting Procedures Act, 1950. On the

other hand, the GAO is provided with powers and duties

broadly similar to those outlined in the previous sections

of this chapter. In other countries, government audit

departments would not be allowed to audit self-imposed

standards.

Two other agencies also contribute to the function of

financial managment and control. The Fiscal Service of

the Treasury provides facilities for the receipt and payment

of public monies and is also responsible for preparing the

consolidated accounts of the federal Government. The

Office of Management and the Budget (OMB) is responsible

for the supervision, control and administration of the

budget and financial programmes of the Government.

Increasingly the OMB is becoming the major influence in

federal government accounting. As Cate states (p.5):

"...some of the most controversial GAO accounting 'principles'
to which agencies on occasion take such strong exception
are not even GAO inspired. Rather GAO is in the dubious
position, perhaps by choice however, of pushing the agencies
towards compliance with requirements that are set forth by
OMB and/or federal statutes.... GAO is in many respects
an accounting translation of OMB policy and procedures."

Translation or not of OMB policies, the position is still

clear: the GAO has a conflict of interest.

Since the early 1970s the GAO has stressed the importance

of independent reviews of efficiency and effectiveness -
the 'program results review'. A 1972 GAO publication
entitled 'Standards for Audit of Government Organizations,
Programs, Activities and Functions' (called the yellow
book) acknowledged an expanded audit role within the public
sector. In addition to establishing standards to improve
the scope of audits, the yellow book defined the objectives
of auditing as reviewing:

(a)   financial operations and compliance with
       applicable laws and regulations;

(b)   economy and efficiency of management practices;
       and

(c)   the effectiveness of programmes in achieving
       a desired level of results.

The standards set forth in this and subsequent publications
are applicable to the audits of all levels of Government.
Indeed one major motive behind the publication of the yellow
book was to encourage auditors of state and local Governments,
over whom the Comptroller General has no authority, to
elevate their own level of practice. Standards at these
levels of Government can best be described as variable.
Writing in 1981, Granhof and Beerman stated that (p.353):

"The requirements for the performance-type audit set forth
in the 'standards' (yellow book) have not yet, however,
been incorporated in the official pronouncements of the
American Institute of Certified Public Accountants, the
organization of independent professional auditors, nor in
those of the National Council on Government Accounting, a
group which has primary responsibility for developing
accounting and auditing principles and standards for
municipalities. With some notable exceptions, few cities
have either established formal requirements for evaluation
of performance by independent auditors (or have developed
the organizational capability of conducting them internally).
Auditors are frequently required to report any violation
of existing laws or regulations, as well as any clear
instances of waste or inefficiency, but their efforts have
been predominantly orientated toward the verification of
financial statements."

In 1978 the GAO published an Exposure Draft, 'Comprehensive

Approach For Planning and Conducting A Program Results

Review' in which the US approach is defined (p.6):

"Program results review

A program results review is a process or approach by which
qualified individuals can determine the level of program
effectiveness and, if necessary, identify areas for improved
program performance.

A program results review extends beyond traditional audit
theory into the realm of activities commonly known as
evaluation and analysis. Program results review activities
are neither constrained to the conventional audit of
information and control systems nor as pervasive as the
wide range of activities associated with evaluation and
analysis. A program results review incorporates three
objectives:

- assessing the adequacy of management's system for
  measuring effectiveness;

-    determining whether a program satisfactorily achieves
     a desired level of program results;

-    identifying causes that inhibit satisfactory performance."

With the GAO audit approach both the structures and the

process of an effective measurement system are reviewed.

The structure describes what the system is and the process

describes what the system does. Effectiveness measurement

systems are expected to consist of three structural components

and two operational/process activities. These five elements

are shown in Figure 4.

Whilst stressing the desirability of performance indicators

the GAO recognizes that it is not always practicable

to express program objectives in detail and that reasonable

surrogates or performance indicators should be developed.

The auditor is required to satisfy himself of the adequacy

of the management's effectiveness measurement system

(managers being generally free to determine effectiveness

by whatever means they believe to be appropriate).

If a measurement system is found to be inadequate, the review

team must not only propose recommendations to correct the

deficiency but also expand the scope of their review

assignment. This expansion of the audit role, to that of

Figure 4   Elements of an effectiveness measurement system

I.   STRUCTURAL COMPONEMENTS:

    A.   Performance Indicators — quantifiable expressions of program objectives

    B.   Data Source — base from which information about performance indicators can be obtained

    C.   Performance Standards — desired level of achievement force performance indicator.

II.   PROCESS ACTIVITIES

    A.   Data Collection Process — collecting performance indicator data from the data source

    B.   Comparison Process — comparing the actual status of a performance indicator with the appropriate performance standard to determine extent of program effectiveness.

(Source: 'Comprehensive Approach For Planning and Conducting A Program Results Review', G A O, June 1978, p.10)

an 'in-depth' review, is very much atypical of the GAO

approach. In many respects these 'in-depth' investigations

are ad hoc. Morse, a former GAO director, provided the

following guidelines as to when detailed investigations

are called for (p.43):

"Some of the specific factors which the alert auditor should
consider in assessing the management control system and
identifying problem areas warranting more detailed audit
include the following:

1.   The use by management of standards or goals for judging
      the accomplishment, productivity, efficiency or use
      of goods or services.

2.   Lack of clarity in written instructions which may result
      in misunderstandings, inconsistent applications,
      unacceptable deviations in what was wanted and the
      like.

3.   Capabilities of personnel to perform their assignments.

4.   Failures to accept responsibility.

5.   Duplication of effort.

6.   Improper or wasteful use of funds.

7.   Cumbersome or extravagant organizational patterns.

8.   Ineffective or wasteful use of employees and physical
      resources.

9.   Work backlogs."

Sweden

Sweden has been included in this chapter for two reasons.

Firstly it was the first European country to adopt formally

effectiveness auditing. Secondly, there are some
characteristic features of its central administration
which are worthy of consideration.

In Sweden the control of legality is separated in principle
from economic control. Parliament's control of administrative
legality is undertaken by the Parliamentary Ombudsman, an
institution which has its counterpart in other countries,
e.g. in Israel. On behalf of the Government, administrative
legality is scrutinized by the Chancellor of Justice. Both
of these institutions maintain contact to ensure that, as
a rule, they do not consider the same matter simultaneously.
Legality control involves ensuring that laws and other
statutes are applied in a proper manner.

Economic control is exercised separately by two main auditing
bodies. For Parliament auditing is carried out by the
Parliamentary Auditors, consisting of twelve Members of
Parliament elected for one year at a time. In many respects
their role is similar to our own Public Accounts Committee.
The difference is, though, that the twelve Members of
Parliament, so elected, have a permanent secretariat of
about twenty whose chief concern is with effectiveness
auditing. The main burden of central administrative auditing
is carried out by the National Audit Bureau (NAB). The

NAB carry out both financial auditing and effectiveness

auditing which they see as complementary. They are defined

by Berggren, the Auditor General of Sweden, as follows

(p.5):

"Financial auditing of a Government agency shall result in
a professional and impartial opinion on the agency's
financial statement and records.

Effectiveness auditing in the central administration involves
examining the effectiveness and productivity of an agency
or an activity. One purpose of this is to check that
activities are being carried out in a functional, systematic
and economically satisfactory way. Effectiveness auditing
should also give rise to ideas and incentives for
improvements at all levels of the central administration.
The ultimate goal of the audit is to promote effectivenss
in public administration."

The link between financial auditing and effectiveness

auditing is provided by an examination of the systems of

internal control which are expected to provide management

with both accounting and non-accounting information.

An assessment of an agency's effectiveness starts with three

questions (Berggren, p.14):

"To what extent do the effects of activities agree with
their goals?
How well is an agency run?
Is productivity satisfactory?"

On the basis of the answers to these questions effectiveness auditing is directed at three aspects, as illustrated in

Figure 5 and defined by Berggren, (p.14):

"Goal analysis, which involves examining how the agency
interprets and operationalizes the intentions of Parliament
and Government, how it arranges the strategic planning of
its own activity and how external effects are followed up.
This aspect also includes analyses of an agency's external
relations (demands, interested parties and needs).

Audit of operations, which involves examining an agency's
production. An examination of an agency's performances is
here linked as far as possible with an examination of the
actual effects that are generated. Resource utilization
is also examined in this context.

Audit of systems, which involves examining the agency's
control system, its organization and administrative support
functions. Planning for the short and medium term, budgeting
and followups are included in the framework for this
examination."

Only in two of the countries reviewed, Canada and the United

States of America, has there been any significant private

sector involvement in VFM audit and consultancy assignments.

With increasing opportunities for UK firms to undertake

similar assignments, valuable lessons can be learned from

both public and private sector experience in other countries.

The bibliography at the end of the book contains supplementary

references to these specifically referred to at the end of

individual chapters.

Figure 5   The aspects of an effectiveness examination

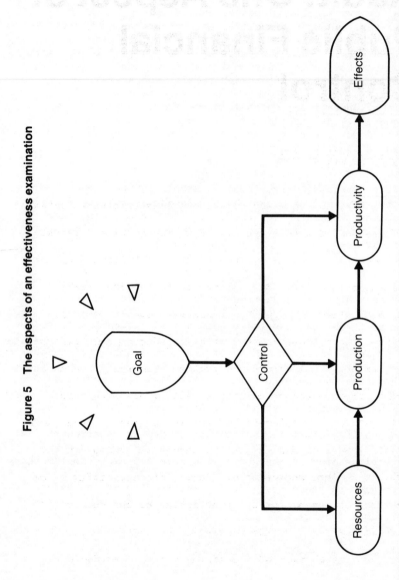

(Source: G. Rune Berggren, 'Effectiveness auditing in Sweden's central government administration', p.15.   Unpublished paper, Swedish National Audit Bureau.)

6
Audit: One Aspect of Public Financial Control

Public Accountability

This chapter is concerned with the present status of external

auditing in the public sector. How successful are recent

developments in auditing, such as the establishment of the

Audit Commission and the passing of the National Audit

Act, 1983, likely to be? Their success will be partially

dependent upon those charged with introducing such reforms

and partially by a more basic problem concerning the parallel

need to improve accountability at all levels within the

public sector. Parliament, ministers, permanent secretaries

and all levels of management throughout the public sector

ought to be more accountable. Public accountability is an

important component for the functioning of our democratic

political system. Public sector accountability means that

those who are charged with drafting and/or carrying out

policy should be obliged to give an explanation of their

actions to their electorate. The very notion of

accountability could give rise to a whole book on its

own.[1]

Audit is an ex post event and improvements in this important

function may be of little long-term value if these are not

coupled with more general reforms of the accountability of

government. As Heald states, (p.155):

"The growth in the public sector, both in terms of its scale
and the diversity of its scale and the diversity of its
activities, has outstretched the traditional machinery of
public accountability, heavily dependent upon the formal
relationship between the executive and the legislative.
There have emerged alternative views of what accountability
entails, involving different answers to both the substance
and form of the account. The conceptions of accountability
which now dominate the debate are political accountability,
managerial accountability and legal accountability."

In developing his argument Heald incorporates his three

classifications with the nine types of accountability

distinguished by Smith in a paper that appeared in the

Policy Studies Journal in 1980. Both views are incorporated

in Figure 6. Sociologists and political scientists have

devoted much time in developing a variety of theories on

the determination of public sector expenditure. They have

been concerned with many aspects of accountability listed

under Division I and III. Likewise, economists have discussed

Figure 6: Conceptions of Public Sector Accountability

Division	Sub-division	
I Political Accountability	(a) Constitutional Accountability	– the hallmark of parliamentary systems
	(b) Decentralized Accountability	– the devolution of control and accountability e.g. to local authorities
	(c) Consultative Accountability	– the involvement of 'interested parties' and 'pressure groups'
II Managerial Accountability	(a) Commercial Accountability	– publicly owned organizations, financed by user charges and not by budgetary appropriations
	(b) Resource Accountability	– adopting managerial practices that will promote the efficiency and effectiveness of non-commercial entities; by the establishment of an appropriate budgetary control framework
	(c) Professional Accountability	– self-regulation by professional groups employed in the public sector
III Legal Accountability	(a) Judicial Accountability	– a review of executive actions at the instigation of an aggrieved individual; decisions should not be ultra vires those required by statute
	(b) Quasi-judicial Accountability	– the control of administrative discretion; e.g. by review tribunals
	(c) Procedural Accountability	– a review of decisions by an external agency, usually by an ombudsman.

at length technical aspects of economic policy, particularly
macro-economic policy. They have been concerned with
certain aspects of accountability listed under Divisions I
and II. However, accountants who also ought to be
particularly concerned with the concepts of accountability
listed under Divisions I and II have not traditionally
played a major role. Whilst the accountancy profession
has contributed, to a limited extent, to improving commercial
and professional accountability, further work needs to be
carried out in order to improve the present level of
constitutional, decentralized and resource concepts of
accountability.

Whilst the concern of this monograph is with VFM auditing,
it has to be realized that improvements in this area alone
are insufficient. There is a need for reform on a broader
front. Indeed, it may be that many of the present reforms
affecting the scope of the audit will lose their impact if
there are not also reforms which lead to improvements in
the quality of management information. Accountability
will need to be judged on the basis of data provided by
the management information system. (Remember that the
function of the VFM auditor is to assess and report on
managements' efforts to develop effective programmes as
efficiently as possible.) The development of VFM auditing

should lead to improved accountability in the public sector.

However, such improvement will be slow since the auditor

will be reporting upon past events and present practices.

If an auditor produces an adverse report improvements will

have to be made by management. Such an approach to improving

management information systems is at best piecemeal.

Consistency between different organizations will be lost

and problems of comparability between different programmes

will remain. A major reform of public sector accountability

is long overdue and needs to start from the top down: that

is, with constitutional accountability.

A few questions from the First Report of the Procedure

Committee, Session 1977/78, illustrate the need for a

top-down approach to reform. Paragraph 8.2 states:

"It is clear to us that the present procedures of the House
are inadequate for control over public expenditure and
ensuring that money is effectively spent. The House as a
whole has long since ceased to exercise detailed control
over expenditure in any but the formal sense of voting the
annual estimates and approving the Consolidated Fund and
Appropriation Bills. The time which was set aside by the
House for the consideration of supply is now rarely used
for purposes even tenuously connected with public expenditure.
When motions of a financial character are put before the
House for consideration on Supply days they are for the
most part vehicles for general debate and not regarded as
opportunities for detailed examination of the Executive's
expenditure proposals...."

Presumably one reason for the lack of detailed examination

is because of the present format by which expenditure details
are presented to the House. Another reason concerns the
functioning of committees and the role of the Comptroller
and Auditor General. Paragraph 8.3 states:

"Over the years the House has attempted to devise suitable
methods for the control of public expenditure. Its longest
method is the Public Accounts Committee.... Its remit is,
however, too limited both in breadth and depth and its
control of expenditure is 'post-hoc'. The Expenditure
Committee, on the other hand, is empowered to consider the
estimates and other expenditure papers... the Expenditure
Committee has doubts about whether the information provided
by the Executive is sufficient to enable it to perform its
functions effectively."

The then chairman of the Public Accounts Committee (PAC),
Joel Barnett, told the Procedure Committee that the remit
given to the PAC and the Comptroller and Auditor General
was inadequate. He complained that the PAC did not have
authority over many bodies that were in receipt of state
aid. He contrasted this with the position in the private
sector where a bank had control over the loans that it
made. With respect to the Exchequer and Audit Department
he stated that the staff did:

"... a marvellous and painstaking job, it was a shocking
thing (that)... the range of qualification is limited in
numbers and also limited in scope."

Their American equivalents were:

"... very much better fitted to the contemporary age, very much better fitted to give advice to Members of Parliament..."

Dr. E.L. Normanton, an auditor with the United Nations, was also interviewed. He stated that:

"... in the field of public accountability institutions, procedures and thinking generally have not kept pace with events."

He went on to state that:

"... the status of British Auditors was fixed at a level in the public service which was unquestionably the lowest of any majority in the Western World."

It is against this background that recent developments have to be judged. Their hopes for success will be in spite of the existing framework of public sector accountability. As Edward Du Cann stated to the Procedure Committee:

"I would myself emphatically not accept that there is any room for criticism of what the PAC does do, still less of the work of the Comptroller and Auditor General and his staff do on behalf of Parliament. If there is a fault in the situation, and there is a grievous fault, in my view the fault is Parliament's...."

National Audit Act 1983

Prior to the passing of the National Audit Act 1983, the

main legislation concerned with the external audit of

central Government was the Exchequer and Audit Departments

Act 1866, as amended by the 1921 Act. The C&AG has generally

been appointed from outside of the Exchequer and Audit

Department, invariably someone who has previously served

in the Treasury, and not a professional auditor or accountant.

Indeed it is only since 1975 that all new entrants to the

Exchequer and Audit Department have been required to take,

and pass, a professional qualifation. They are now required

to sit the examinations of the Chartered Institute of

Public Finance and Accountancy. As stated in Chapter 1,

the C&AG is appointed by the Crown, on the advice of the

Prime Minister. He can only be dismissed if a motion to

that effect is passed by both Houses of Parliament.

The Exchequer and Audit Department perform both financial

and VFM audits. In theory, though not always in practice,

the 1866 Act required a 100% audit of all transactions.

The 1921 Act revoked this unworkable requirement and so

indirectly condoned the concept of test auditing and, in

more recent times, the adoption of a systems-based audit.

The objectives of the statutory audit are threefold. They

are to check that funds provided by Parliament have been

spent as intended, that unlawful or irregular payments

have been made and that the figures are correct. Because

the expenditure of many departments runs into hundreds of

millions of pounds it is therefore a major audit task to

check that the accounting and financial control systems

underlying reported expenditure are both efficient and

accurate.

According to Sir Douglas Henley, a former C&AG (p.215):

"Value-for-money audit has been commonly used in the UK as
a convenient description of the evolving interests and work
of E&AD over many decades, with its origin sometimes
pinpointed in the year 1888 when there was an interesting
confrontation between the C&AG and the Army Council over a
little matter of contracts for Army ribbon, from which the
former emerged the winner. The argument was whether the
C&AG was within his rights in extending his examination of
Army expenditure beyond the accepted matters of conformity
with Parliamentary authorization into the area of economy
in contracts.... Over the succeeding century the C&AG has
developed the application of value for money into many
aspects of the financial management of Government departments,
with a marked acceleration in scale and coverage from the
early 1950s, as the great post-war surge in Government
activity and the corresponding expenditure programmes
gathered weight."

Whilst accepting that the Exchequer and Audit Department

has in recent times devoted greater attention to VFM auditing,

little else is known. The audit practices and philosophy

that underlie the E&AD's approach to VFM auditing remain

shrouded by a veil of secrecy. This is in stark contrast

to the practice adopted by the five countries reviewed in

the previous chapter. According to Henley (p.217):

"In the UK ... value-for-money audit has come to describe
a wide variety of enquiries into Central Government
operations, including the development and production of
military equipment; the building of hospitals, factories
and offices; the application of agricultural and industrial
assistance; the design and installation of computer systems;
charging policies for Government services; use and disposal
of land; control of civil service manpower. The C&AG's
reports have concentrated on financial management in the
broadest sense, including the management of contracts.
They have also raised matters of organization, and more
recently the control of civil service manpower. They have
not, however, extended into the field of operational research
or work study."

The C&AG's annual report, which accompanies the approved

Estimates submitted to the House of Commons, is fairly short

when one considers that it covers the whole of Central

Government expenditure. It covers aspects of both financial

and VFM audit and, though short and to the point, it is

devoid of any information that would enable a researcher

to gauge the quality and scope of the work carried out.

One hundred and fourteen years after the passing of the

1866 Act the Government issued a green paper (Cmnd 7845,

March 1980) on the role of the C&AG. This was followed by

the Public Account Committee's first special report, session

1980-81 and the Government's response to that report (Cmnd

8323). These three documents provided, for the first time

in over a century, a summary of the various arguments on

the subject of the national audit office.

Paragraph 64 of the Green Paper welcomed views from the

Parliamentary Committees and other interested bodies and

individuals on the Government's views, which were summarized

as follows:

"(a)   The role of the C&AG should be
        (i) to provide a basic financial and regularity
            audit of departmental accounts;
       (ii) to undertake an examination of the economy and
            efficiency with which public funds are spent;
            and
      (iii) in appropriate cases, to investigate the
            effectiveness of programmes and projects in
            meeting established policy goals.

 (b)   The effective working relationship between the C&AG
       and the PAC should be preserved.

 (c)   In the case of non-departmental bodies an important
       objective of the C&AG's examination should be to
       review the effectiveness of the arrangements under
       which Ministers monitor and control the payment of
       public funds to such bodies.

 (d)   Decisions whether to provide for C&AG audit or
       inspection of such bodies need to be taken case by
       case. The C&AG should not cover the nationalized
       industries.

 (e)   Certain powers of direction available to the Treasury
       in the E&AD Acts are obsolete and could be removed
       in any new legislation.

 (f)   The Government are prepared to consider alternative
       arrangements for controlling the budget of the C&AG,
       but the implications for the staff of E&AD would
       need to be considered.

 (g)   The independence of the C&AG of both the Executive
       and Parliament should be reaffirmed and there should
       be no change in his status as an office holder under
       the Crown."

The PAC's response to this Green Paper came in the form of

a three-volume report in February 1981:   The First Special

Report from the Committee of Public Accounts, Session 1980-

81 (HC 115), 'The Role of the Comptroller and Auditor General'.

Whilst agreeing with the general views expressed in paragraph

64(a) above, the PAC proposed more radical changes.   Paragraph

8.1 stated:

"... the present legislation is out of date and does not
reflect the nature of the audit at present carried out by
the C&AG. More importantly, it is essential to make
statutory provision for a framework of public audit in
this country sufficient to ensure accountability to
Parliament for the wider range of public expenditure now
and in the future."

The specific proposals of the PAC were set out in paragraph
8.10 to 8.16:

"8.10.   We therefore recommend:

(a)   Where a grant financed body is mainly supported from
        public funds, the C&AG should have the right to audit
        the accounts of that body and those accounts should
        be laid before Parliament; (paragraph 3.8).

(b)   In the case of other non-departmental bodies the C&AG
        should have access to the body's books and records
        and should report to the House of Commons the results
        of his examination (paragraph 3.10).

(c)   The present arrangements for the financial audit of
        the nationalized industries and other public
        corporations including the NEB and BNOC should
        continue, but the C&AG should have access to the
        books and records of those bodies to enable him to
        report to the House of Commons (paragraph 4.16 -
        4.19).

(d)   It should be a condition of all grants or loans of
        money voted by Parliament to privately-owned companies
        or other bodies whether of a commercial nature or
        not that the C&AG should have access where he considers
        it necessary, to the books and records of those
        bodies (paragraph 4.20).

(e)   The present arrangements for the audit of local
        authorities in England and Wales by the District
        Auditor or an approved auditor should continue, but
        responsibility for approving the appointment of the
        approved auditors should be transferred from the
        Secretary of State for the Environment to the Chief
        Inspector for Local Government External Audit. The
        Chief Inspector should continue to make an annual
        report on matters arising from the auditors' reports.
        The staff of the District Audit Service should be
        transferred from the Department of the Environment
        to the C&AG and the C&AG should report to Parliament
        on general matters arising out of the audit of local
        authorities in England and Wales (paragraphs 5.34,
        5.35 and 5.36).

(f)   Consideration should be given to transferring the
        functions of the Commission for Local Authority
        Accounts in Scotland to the C&AG (paragraph 5.40).

(g)   The general audit of Health Authorities should be
        transferred from the Health Departments to the C&AG
        (paragraph 6.9).

(h)   We make no recommendations at present for changes in
        the role of the C&AG for Northern Ireland (paragraph
        1.8).

A National Audit Office

8.11.   There should be a national audit office to carry
out the functions of the C&AG (paragraph 7.1).

8.12.   The costs of the national audit office should be
borne on the Vote of the House of Commons (paragraphs 7.8
and 7.9).

8.13.   There should be a separate Vote for the national
audit office (paragraph 7.9).

8.14.   Legislation should provide for the establishment of
a Public Accounts Commission, consisting of Members of the
House of Commons appointed by resolution of the House of
Commons, including the Chairman of the Committee of Public
Accounts.   The functions of that Commission should be:

  (a)   to appoint the Chief Inspector of Local Government
         External Audit;
  (b)   to appoint the staff of the national audit office;
  (c)   to determine the staff numbers of the national
         audit office, their remuneration and other terms
         and conditions of service;
  (d)   to prepare an annual estimate of the national
         audit office;
  (e)   to appoint an accounting officer responsible for
         accounting for the sums paid out of money for the
         national audit office; (paragraph 7.10)

8.15.   The C & AG should become the head of the national
audit office.   The existing staff of E&AD and the District
Audit Service should be transferred to the national audit
office (paragraph 7.8 - 7.10).

8.16.   Provision should be made in the new audit legislation
for the Treasury to appoint the auditors of the national
audit office (paragraph 7.31)."

Paragraph 8.16 was to cover the fact that there is, at

present, no statutory provision for the audit of the E&AD.

The department is audited by the Permanent Secretary to

the Treasury.

The Government's response to the PAC's proposals came in

July 1981 (Cmnd 8323).   It was not in favour of giving the

C&AG an extended remit.   Paragraph 6 stated:

"It remains the Government's view that it would be useful
to introduce legislation to provide an up-to-date prescription
of the C&AG's functions.   But this is not a pressing need.

Experience of the past two years suggests that the existing
legislation need not in fact inhibit further desirable
changes in the work of the C&AG and the PAC...."

There the debate rested until Norman St John Stevas brought

a private member's bill to the House. After a stormy

passage, and much pruning, this bill emerged as the National

Audit Act, 1983. The Act, which is in three parts, came

into force on 1 January 1984. Part I of the Act provides

that the C&AG shall be an officer of the House of Commons.

This move had been opposed by the government (Cmnd 8323,

paragraph 26). A body, known as The Public Accounts

Commission, is to be established to oversee the provisions

of this Act. The composition of this Commission will be

as follows:

(a)   the Member of the House of Commons who is for the time

       being the Chairman of the Committee of Public Accounts;

(b)   the Leader of the House of Commons; and

(c)   seven other Members of the House of Commons appointed

       by the House, none of whom shall be a Minister of the

       Crown.

The Commission will, from time to time, report to the House.

There is to be a new title given to the C&AG's department:

The National Audit Office. All those currently employed in

the Exchequer and Audit Department will receive an offer of

employment in the new department. The C&AG will each year

present to the House of Commons the estimated operating

costs of his department. Paragraph 4(2) states:

"The Comptroller and Auditor General shall for the financial
year ending 31 March 1984 and for each subsequent financial
year prepare an estimate of the expenses of the National
Audit Office; and the Commission shall examine that estimate
and lay it before the House of Commons with such modifications,
if any, as the Commission sees fit."

Part II of the Act is devoted to Economy, Efficiency and

Effectiveness Examinations. Such investigations are still

to be primarily directed at those bodies that are presently

audited by the C&AG. Paragraph 7 states, in part:

"(1)   If the Comptroller and Auditor General has reasonable
cause to believe that any authority or body to which this
section applies has in any of its financial years received
more than half its income from public funds he may carry
out an examination into the economy, efficiency and
effectiveness with which it has in that year used its
resources in discharging its functions.

(2)   Subsection (1) above shall not be construed as
entitling the Comptroller and Auditor General to question
the merits of the policy objectives of any authority or
body in respect of which an examination is carried out."

Specifically excluded from the provisions of this paragraph

are over twenty nationalized industries and other public

bodies. These are listed in Schedule 4 of the Act.

Part III of the Act is entitled Miscellaneous and

Supplementary. Paragraphs 11 and 12 remove the power of

the Treasury to give, in certain circumstances, directives

to the C&AG. Though there is no record of this power ever

being exercised, this is an important amendment of principle.

The National Audit Act 1983 is not as radical as might have

been hoped for. Little was known about the philosophy and

approaches adopted by the (now to be replaced) E&AD. This

practice of non-disclosure seems likely to continue with the

establishment of the National Audit Office. Such secrecy

is, as previously stated, in stark contrast to the approach

adopted in very many other countries.

The Audit Commission

The Local Government Finance Act 1982 established the Audit

Commission for Local Authorities in England and Wales (the

Commission). Appendix A provides a summary of the main

provisions of Part III of this Act which fundamentally

changed the structure of the external audit of local

authorities in England and Wales.

The Commission came into being on 1 April 1983; it has two

main responsibilities:

(1) To secure continued integrity of Local Government, so
that confidence in the institutions of government is not
eroded by concerns over fraud and corruption.

(2) To help authorities improve the returns on the £25
billion+ invested annually in goods and services, as
required by Section 15, viz:

"An auditor shall by examination of the accounts and
otherwise satisfy himself ... that the body whose accounts
are being audited has proper arrangements for securing
economy, efficiency and effectiveness in the use of its
resources."

The Commission has a chairman and thirteen members, who
represent the interests of rate-payers, authorities,
employees and accountants. The day-to-day operation of
the Commission rests with its Controller. Currently the
Commission is appointing auditors to local authorities for
the audit of the accounts for the financial year 1984.
The authorities covered by the Commission are:

- the GLC and the 32 London Boroughs;

- 89 Countries and Metropolitan Districts;

- 333 Non-Metropolitan Districts;

- 7 Passenger Transport Executives;

- 8,000 Towns and Parishes;

- 250 Internal Drainage Boards;

- 140 other Local Government Bodies.

At present the majority (70%) of audit appointments will stay with the District Audit Service, the balance (30%) going to private sector firms approved by the Commission. All appointments will normally last for five years subject to satisfactory performance, and it is intended that future appointments will increase the share of the private sector. This transfer of work to the private sector reflects the Commission's organization structure and operating style, which is designed to encourage a sense of partnership between the District Audit Service and private sector firms, accountants and consultants, the Commission and local authorities. The Commission will be buying in services rather than providing them internally.

The Commission regards VFM audit as being particularly important. Each authority will receive an 'Authority Profile' which will identify the main value for money issues that it needs to resolve. This report will summarize the available comparative statistics and trend information relevant to the authority, and draw attention to what appear to be main value for money issues to be investigated in the course of the audit. Every year, the Commission intends to identify specific services or costs. For the audit of financial year 1984 the focus will be on:

- the overall arrangements for securing economy, efficiency
  and effectiveness,
- polytechnics and colleges of further education,
- police civilianization,
- school meals,
- refuse collection,
- purchasing, and
- planning and development.

Each of these areas is termed a 'flavour of the year' and
each audit is expected to include three or four VFM projects
covering some of the above 'flavours'.

Figure 7 provides an overview of the proposed VFM projects
for the financial years 1984 to 1986. In some cases the
Commission would expect economy and effectiveness to go
hand in hand, e.g. in introducing a higher proportion of
civilians into the police force or boarding out a higher
proportion of children in care. In endeavouring to secure
increased returns on the investment managed by local
government the Commission realizes that without effective
local leadership and initiative, real progress is unlikely.
The Commission considers that recent cost reduction pressures
on local authorities have been largely ineffective. In
their words:[2]

Figure 7   Overview of proposed audit commission value for money work

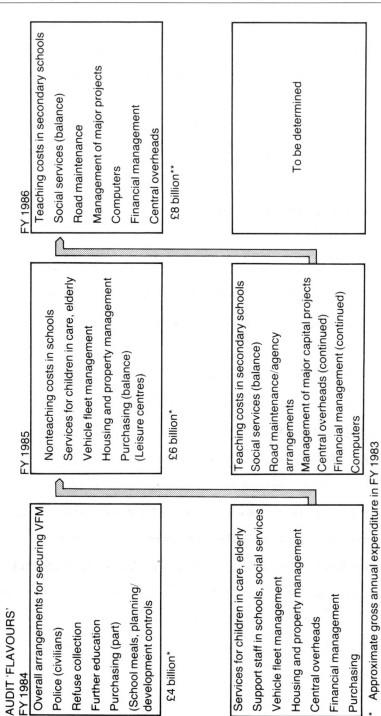

AUDIT 'FLAVOURS'

FY 1984

Overall arrangements for securing VFM
Police (civilians)
Refuse collection
Further education
Purchasing (part)
(School meals, planning/
development controls)

£4 billion*

Services for children in care, elderly
Support staff in schools, social services
Vehicle fleet management
Housing and property management
Central overheads
Financial management
Purchasing

FY 1985

Nonteaching costs in schools
Services for children in care, elderly
Vehicle fleet management
Housing and property management
Purchasing (balance)
(Leisure centres)

£6 billion*

Teaching costs in secondary schools
Social services (balance)
Road maintenance/agency
arrangements
Management of major capital projects
Central overheads (continued)
Financial management (continued)
Computers

FY 1986

Teaching costs in secondary schools
Social services (balance)
Road maintenance
Management of major projects
Computers
Financial management
Central overheads

£8 billion**

To be determined

* Approximate gross annual expenditure in FY 1983
** Excluded loan charges of over £4.5 billion/year

"... conversations with the members and senior officers of
local authorities ... suggests that the kind of behaviour
patterns shown in the Exhibit (here reproduced as Figure 8)
are more frequent. And for good reasons:

- irresponsibility has been encouraged in that authorities
  have been able to 'blame' Central Government rather than
  set their own houses in order (literally, as well as
  figuratively);

- defensive attitudes have become entrenched; local
  authorities (both officers and members) are poised to
  resist all initiatives however well intentioned as
  'threats to local democracy': so constructive action
  is unlikely."

The Commission hopes to motivate authorities to make

improvements by helping them to help themselves.

Specifically, the Commission sees its mission as being

to:(3)

"(1)   Identify specific local opportunities to improve
value for money, in the course of the annual audit effort
- by reference to other steps that already have been taken
successfully in other authorities facing similar problems.

(2)   Promote good management practice, by documenting
achievements and training auditors to spot potential
improvements, and publishing the results of Special Studies.

(3)   Encourage - even promote - action, through (auditors')
reports to officers and members, management letters to the
authority and (if necessary) reports in the public interest.

(4)   Monitor implementation performance during annual audits,
drawing attention as required to any shortfall.

(5)   Co-ordinate the efforts of related organizations...."

Figure 9 shows the proposed organization structure of the

Figure 8   Trends in real local government expenditure*, 1971–1983

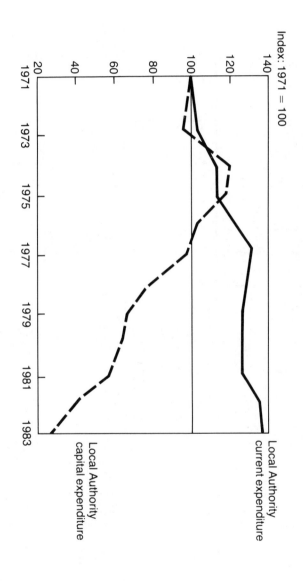

Index: 1971 = 100

Local Authority
current expenditure

Local Authority
capital expenditure

* Deflated by income from employment index (current expenditure) and index of prices for domestic fixed capital formation

(Source: DOE; Audit Commission analysis of National Accounts Statistics,
Table 8.)

VMA–L

Figure 9   Audit Commission: proposed organization structure

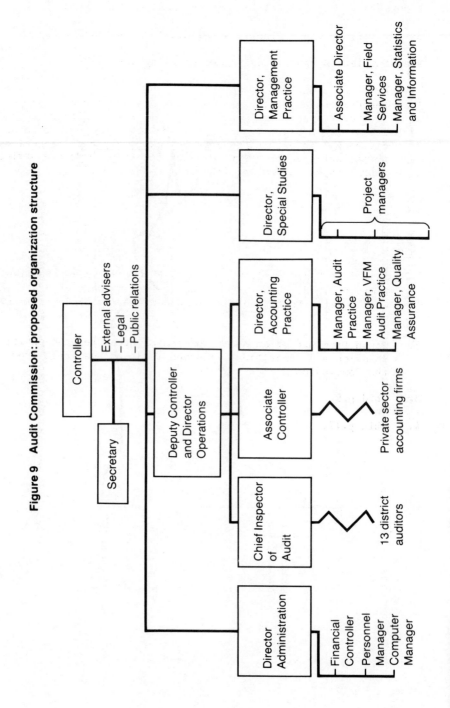

Commission. The Commission does not believe that it would

be fruitful to gauge simply individual local authority's

spending levels against aggregate spending levels[4]:

"... the Commission will not be judging its performance against
local authority spending levels since this would be incompatible
with its stated mission of helping authorities to improve returns
on their annual investment and, in any case, any cost reductions
will not be achieved by the Commission but by members and officers
of authorities demonstrating 'the will to manage'."

Notes

1.   Indeed it has: Bird, P, Accountability, Haymarket Publishing
      Limited, 1973. However the author is not aware of a single
      book devoted to the notion of accountability of Government.

2.   Taken from p.8 of an Audit Commission press release entitled
      'Mission and Priorities'. Issued 1983 and available from
      the Commission's Press Officer.

3.   Ibid p.9.

4.   Ibid p.17.

7
Concluding
Comments

Value for money is of concern to all those involved with
the public sector; that is the politicians and administrators
who manage its various organizations, and the public who
both contribute to and benefit from the services they
provide. It is achieved by planning, reporting upon and
reviewing performance on the basis of clear, unambiguous
statements of policy objectives. Value for money is therefore
an expression of the economy, the efficiency and the
effectiveness with which all institutions, large and small,
operate in the public sector.

The problem is though, that all those involved in either
the provision or receipt of services from public sector
institutions do not necessarily have homogeneous expectations.
Politicians, with re-election always in mind, look to a
short-term horizon in which they wish to achieve results.
Administrators are more concerned with longer term success.
Members of the public are in the schizophrenic position

of, on the one hand, demanding better provision and quality
of services whilst, on the other hand, not wishing to make
additional contributions. Conflict is ever present at all
levels of Government. For example, the Treasury gauges
its success in causing Central Government departments and
local authorities to keep within defined public expenditure
plans, and the Nationalized Industries within their external
financing limits. This is a crude approach to forcing
organizations to improve upon their efficiency.

Such an overly strong emphasis on cash control is too
often at the expense of organizational performance.
Management has little incentive to innovate and develop
its own plans. There is a need for a more systematic and
rational approach to the management and provision of public
sector services - one that is not the result of some 'broad
brush' and ad hoc enquiry. Such an approach would involve
the external auditor in reporting on management's efforts
to secure value for money. The public sector auditor has
responsibilities that go beyond the responsibility of
auditors in the private sector.

The Future

VFM auditing is one means of ensuring that public sector

organizations are called to account for their actions.
Since the term 'value for money' has assumed a wide and
ambiguous meaning it was necessary in Chapter 2 to define
its three component terms: Economy, Efficiency and
Effectiveness. All three terms are now commonplace in the
literature. In the past certain aspects of economy and
efficiency have been covered during the course of the
regularity audit. For example, an inadquate billing and/or
payment procedure could materially affect an organization's
cash flow position. However, such an approach is clearly
limited in scope.

The greatest challenge to the auditing profession, as VFM
auditing becomes a regular exercise for many public sector
organizations, is concerned with the assessment of
effectiveness. As yet, the development of performance
indicators, whereby effectiveness can be gauged, is in a
relative stage of infancy. It is also a politically
sensitive subject littered with pitfalls. Lessons learned
from the experience built up in other countries is a valuable
but insufficient source of guidance. Much more, by way of
research, needs to be undertaken. The auditor will have
to learn new skills and seek the services of non-accounting
specialists.

It is the auditors duty to press for the development of

clear objectives, for the adoption of suitable performance

measures and for the implementation of timely and reliable

management information systems. It is not only the auditor

who needs re-education, the public too needs to be reminded

that, whilst the auditor's role is to seek out areas that

require attention, the responsibility for obtaining value

for money rests with both politicians and management.

A recent report from the Canadian Comprehensive Auditing

Foundation on the role of auditing in municipal administrations

commented on the underdevelopment of VFM auditing in Britain.

It criticized councillors, administrators and auditors.

Councillors were thought to be largely unfamiliar with the

role and capabilities of their auditors and to have little

understanding of financial affairs. Administrators were

in need of improving their dealings with auditors which

were presently described as minimal. Auditors were criticized

for not understanding the nature of councils and for wishing

to avoid controversies.

One of the problems faced by nationalized industries is that,

whilst expected to follow best commercial practice in the

management of their operations, they also have to take

account of the 'public interest' (never defined) in both

their operating and investment decisions. Sherer and Kent

(p.151) note that:

"... the Electricity Act 1957 requires that the electricity
boards 'shall secure as far as possible the extension ...
(of services)... to rural areas' and many other acts
require the nationalized industries to make provisions for
'the welfare, health and safety of persons in their
employment'."

Recently nationalized industries have been requested (in

Cmnd.7131) to develop and publish suitable performance

measures to supplement their more conventional annual

reports. The National Coal Board, for example, now provides

statistics on coal production which detail output and

labour productivity by region. Whilst such improvements

are to be welcomed the fact remains that there is still

only limited public accountability when it comes to reviewing

the efficiency and effectiveness of nationalized industries.

Government ministers, as heads of the various sponsoring

departments, have only an 'arms length' relationship with

industry chairmen. In practice, the Select Committee on

Nationalized Industries and the Select Committee on

Expenditure have, respectively, limited ex post and ex

ante powers of review. It should therefore fall to the

independent external auditor to undertake VFM audit reviews.

However, the lack of enthusiasm of the nationalized industry chairmen is such that the Government would first need to

direct that such exercises be undertaken.

The Layfield Report stated that the performance of local

authorities should be assessed under a number of different

headings, the most important of which were: accountability,

equity and efficiency. The Report stated (p.95):

"... the best way of promoting efficiency and securing value
for money ... is through the dissemination of comprehensive
but intelligble information on the methods employed by local
authorities and the results they achieve."

The Local Government Finance Act 1982, provides the means

by which the Audit Commission and external auditors can

investigate value for money.

It remains to be seen what impact the National Audit Act

1983 will have when it comes to promoting greater

accountability for central government expenditure. It is

insufficient to have administrative efficiency when the

prime requirement of central government expenditure is

that it should be effective; that is, determining whether

programmes or projects have met the policy goals set for

them. Sherer and Kent consider that an effectiveness

audit is both logical and sensible but consider that it is

by no means clear what is or should be the precise scope

of such an audit. They state (p.198):

"The basic difficulty arises because there is no sharp
distinction between the evaluation of decisions taken to
achieve particular government policies and the evaluation
of the policies themselves. The former is concerned with
economic efficiency in its widest sense while the latter
is directly concerned with political judgements."

As discussed in the previous chapter, the present government

is concerned that the C&AG does not take on a political role.

This would seem correct, but it should not preclude the C&AG

from commenting on the effects of such policies. Permanent

heads have significant policy responsibilities in terms of

being responsible for a wide variety of decisions that

directly affect both the choice of programmes adopted and

the strategy to be followed. Permanent heads also play an

important role as policy advisers to ministers and it

would seem quite proper that the policy decisions made by

both ministers and permanent heads should be publicly

reviewed. The C&AG would not be making political judgements,

he would be apolitical as such reviews would not involve

questioning government objectives only the method(s) chosen

to achieve them.

One of the conclusions contained in the 'Review Of The Audit

Act 1958' for the State of Victoria was that (p.40):

"The mechanisms for effectiveness-type reviews of departments
and statutory authorities and the value of the conclusions
of such reviews being public is a matter needing further
urgent study."

This conclusion is equally true in Britain.

Recent changes in legislation have provided the framework

within which VFM auditing is to operate. The professional

accountancy bodies must therefore assist their members in

meeting this challenge. Failure will only lead to further

recriminations that the accountancy profession is, once

again, too slow to change.

Appendix A

Synopsis Of The Local Government Finance Act 1982

Introduction

The Local Government Finance Act 1982 is the most important
piece of legislation affecting the external audit of local
authorities and water authorities in England and Wales since
1972. It also makes changes to the rating powers of local
authorities and to the arrangements for assessing block grant.

Summary of Main Provisions

The Local Government Finance Act 1982 ('the Act') received
the Royal assent on 13 July 1982. There are three main parts
to the Act:

Part I

Abolishes supplementary rates and precepts; requires rates
and precepts to be issued for a complete financial year;

provides for the making of substituted rates and the issue

of substituted precepts; regulates proceedings for

challenging the validity of rates and precepts; makes

further provision with respect to the borrowing powers of

local authorities; and make further provision with respect

to relief from rates in enterprise zones.

Part II

Amends the provisions relating to block grants.

Part III

Makes new provision for auditing the accounts of local

authorities and other public bodies.

Parts I and II are largely self-explanatory and reflect the

Government's continuing intention to reduce local authority

expenditures. The provisions with regard to supplementary

rates were brought about by the change in political complexion

of a number of authorities in 1980, when planned reductions

in spending were re-instated by the new councils with the

aid of supplementary rates and precepts.

The changes in block grant arrangments need to be read in

conjunction with Section 59 of the Local Government Planning

and Land Act, 1980, which gave the Secretary of State
power to adjust local authorities grant entitlements. The
new powers enable the Secretary of State to be more selective
as to which authorities are caught by any grant 'penalties'
introduced under the 1980 Act grant system.

Part III of the Act changes fundamentally the structure of
external audit of local authorities in England and Wales.
The main provisions are as follows:

Section 11 provides for the establishment of an Audit
Commission consisting of not less than 13 nor more than 17
members appointed by the Secretary of State who shall
appoint one of the members to be Chairman and another to
be Deputy Chairman.

Section 12 empowers the Commission to appoint an auditor
or auditors to local authorities.

This section takes away from local authorities power given
them by the Local Government Act 1972 to appoint their own
auditors, who could be either the District Auditor or a firm
approved by the Secretary of State.

Section 13 specifies that the auditor can be either an officer of the Commission or an individual or firm of individuals

possessing a recognized accounting qualification. The

section provides for joint or sole appointments and requires

the Commission to consult authorities before making such

appointments.

The Commission has wide ranging powers under this section

to deploy its own staff (ie. former District audit staff)

and private sector firms in flexible ways. No indication

has yet been given as to what form 'consultation' with

individual authorities will take but the consultation

process will probably allow authorities to express a

preference for a particular firm.

Section 14 requires the Commission to prepare a Code of

Audit Practice prescribing the way in which auditors are

to carry out their functions and embodying best professional

practice with respect to standards, procedures and techniques.

A first draft of the Code of Practice has been prepared by

the Audit Inspectorate and is very much more comprehensive

than the existing code of practice which came into operation

in 1974. A small working group from the private sector is

looking critically at the draft and taking into account the

comments received from a number of firms already involved in

local authority auditing. It is likely that the draft will
be considerably amended, before it is submitted for the
Commission's consideration, with a view to making it less
prescriptive and allowing more scope for the auditor's
professional judgement. The Commission must consult the
Local Authority Associations and the accountancy bodies
about the code and lay it before both Houses of Parliament
for approval.

Section 15 lays down the general duties of the auditor,
which are to satisfy himself that accounts are properly
prepared and the authority has made proper arrangements
for securing economy, efficiency and effectiveness in its
use of resources; and to report on matters of public
interest which come to his attention, whether or not those
matters arise out of the accounts. In carrying out his
duties, the auditor must comply with the Code of Practice.

The wording of this section is very wide and gives the
auditor a great deal of flexibility. For example, he is
to satisfy himself 'by examination of the account and
otherwise' about the authority's practices, procedures and
accounts. The requirement to look at procedures for securing
'effectiveness' is new and in this untried area there will
be considerable scope for different interpretations.

Again, no guidance is contained in the Act about what
constitutes 'the public interest' although there are
precedents from existing reports under the 1972 Act.
Undoubtedly the Commission will be looking for more 'harder
hitting' reports than auditors have been used to preparing
in the past.

Section 16 gives the auditor right of access to all such
documents as appear to him to be necessary for the purposes
of the audit and the right to require people to give
information or explanations.

Section 17 gives 'interested persons' the right to inspect
accounts to be audited and documents relating to those
accounts, to question the auditor on them and to make
objections about possible illegalities or matters on which
the auditor should report.

These two sections broadly repeat existing provision, but
also allow a private sector auditor to deal with objections.

Section 18 requires the auditor on conclusion of the audit
to certify that he has completed the audit and to issue an
opinion on the relevant statements of accounts.

VMA-M

No definition has yet been issued as to what constitutes
'relevant statements of account' but it is possible that
the new regulations to be issued will standardize the form
of published statements (see Section 23 below). In the
past, local Government external auditors have not been
required to give an opinion but the draft Code of Practice
provides for an opinion that the statements 'present fairly'
the financial position of the authority and its income and
expenditure. This will involve more work at the final
audit stage than has been the case in the past.

Section 19 allows the auditor to apply to the court for a
declaration that an item is contrary to law.

Section 20 allows the auditor to certify that items have
not been brought into account that should have been, and
that losses have been incurred or deficiencies caused by
wilful misconduct, and that such sums shall be recovered
by the appropriate persons.

Prior to the Act, only the District Auditor has had the
powers laid down in Sections 19 and 20. In future all
auditors, including those from the private sector, will
have them.

Section 21 authorizes that Commission to prescribe audit

fees. Under existing legislation, fees are prescribed by

the Secretary of State.

Section 22 allows the Commission to direct an auditor to

conduct an extraordinary audit and gives the Secretary of

State power to direct the Commission to cause an

extraordinary audit to be carried out. The power to direct

an extraordinary audit at present rests solely in the

hands of the Secretary of State.

Section 23 gives the Secretary of State power to issue

regulations governing the form, content and publication of

accounts.

The present arrangements are somewhat informal and it is

likely that regulations will be issued to standardize

these matters.

Section 24 entitles electors for an area to inspect and make

copies of accounts and auditors' reports.

This is a new section and supplements the electors' rights

under Section 17.

Section 25 deals with the audits of transactions incidental
to the main purpose of the authority.

For example, trust funds, residents' accounts.

Section 26 requires the Commission to promote studies for
improving economy etc. in services.

There is a new and very wide-ranging provision and reflects
the existing practice in Scotland. It is likely that the
Commission will retain a significant proportion of total
fee income from these studies.

Section 27 requires the Commission to prepare reports on the
impact of statutory provisions and to send copies of such
reports to the Comptroller and Auditor General. The
Commission must also consult with the C&AG on the planning
of such studies.

This is another new field and allows the Commission to
promote studies on, e.g., the effect of Government grant
systems on local authorities generally. The requirement
to send copies of reports to the C&AG has potentially
far-reaching implications, because he can, if he thinks
fit, lay reports before the House of Commons.

Section 28 gives the Commission powers to require people
or bodies to supply it with information.

Section 29 allows the Commission, if requested by an
authority, to make arrangements for certifying grant claims
and for carrying out efficiency studies. It also allows
the Commission to make arrangements for the audit of the
accounts of other bodies connected with local government
if those bodies so request.

The existing law requires the district Auditor to certify
grant claims and it is not yet clear who will carry out
this function in future. It is likely, however, that
private firms will perform some of this work.

Section 30 places certain restrictions on the disclosure of
information obtained by the Commission or by an auditor.

Section 31 makes it clear that the provisions of the Act
also apply to Passenger Transport Executives (PTEs).

Section 32 (and Schedule 4) replace the existing provisions
relating to the audit of water authorities.

At present water authorities are audited under the powers

contained in the Local Government Act 1972. In future,

the auditors will be appointed by the Secretary of State,

although (apart from the requirement to carry out efficiency

studies) the audit requirements are similar to those for

local authorities. Arrangements for the audit of water

authorities are at present under review.

Appendix B

A Checklist Of Areas Which Can Be
Examined To See Their Present Operation
And Possible Future In The Promotion Of
Value For Money
(Source: Holtham and Stewart)

Service

- Motivation

- Leadership

- Ideas about improved service delivery

- Capacity to plan and implement

- Co-operation and accommodation with employees, public etc.

Management Process

- Policy making:

    Corporate working and resource allocation;

    Setting objectives;

    Evaluating alternatives;

    Financial planning;

    Issue analysis and capital project appraisal.

- Programming:

    Budgeting;

    Cash limits, virement and incentives;

    Accountability, framework and structure.

- Review:

    Information and statistics;

    Information and statistics;

    Inter-authority comparisons;

    Monitoring performance - the non-financial information system;

    Review of resource utilization;

    Internal audit - use of;

    Management services - use of.

- Manpower:

    Overall strategy;

    Staff appraisal and reward system;

    Management development;

    Communication within departments.

- Structures:

    Political management - member structure and methods of involvement;

    Corporate management - nature and extent;

    Management within departments - level and nature.

Environment

- Statutory framework

- Public accountability and participation

- External audit

- Central government.

Appendix C

A Checklist For Reviewing Spending
(Source: "Cost Reduction in Public
Authorities – A View", CIPFA, 1979)

1   <u>Employees Expenses</u>

Role of the Trade Unions;

Agency Services;

Staffing Flexibility;

Directly Employed Staff and Contract Employment;

   Operating Expenditure
   Capital Programmes;

Labour Intensive and Plant Intensive Working;

Overtime Working;

Rationalization of Staffing Structures;

Training;

Administration;

Budgeting for Employees Expenses.

2   <u>Premises Expenses</u>

Large Element of Fixed Costs;

Rationalising the Use of Premises;

Repair and Maintenance;

   Reponsibility and Practice;
   Planned Maintenance;

Maintenance of Grounds;

Fuel, Light, Cleaning Materials and Water;

   Tariffs;
   Plant Efficiency;
   Insulation;
   Water;
   Heating and Ventilation;
   Hours and Periods of Use;
   Furniture and Fittings;
   Rent and Rates;
   Design of Buildings.

3   Supplies and Services

Central Supply Organization;

Using Supplies and Services;

   Equipment;
   Provisions;
   Other Supplies;
   Contracted Services;

Contracts;

   Procedure;
   Frequency;
   Form;
   Catchment Area;
   Evaluation;

Stocks and Inventories;

   Stores Organization;
   Stores Records;
   Inventories;
   Computer Methods;

Financing;

    Methods;
    Operating Consequences;
    Budgetary Practices.

4   <u>Transport and Plant Expenses</u>

Co-ordinated Transport Management;

Operation and Deployment;

    Fleet Capacity and Demand;
    Specialist Vehicles and Plant;
    Multi-Purpose Vehicles and Plant Pooling;
    Suitability for Main Purpose;
    Staffing;
    Fuel Facilities;
    Licensing;
    Costing and Records;

Maintenance and Servicing;

    Siting of Depots;
    Spares;
    Tyres;
    Servicing Schedules;

Replacements and Additions;

Allowances to Staff.

5   <u>Establishment Expenses</u>

Printing Arrangements;
Staionery;
Advertising;
Postages;
Telephones;
Travelling, Conference and Subsistence Expenses;
Insurance.

6   <u>Agency Services</u>

Inter-Departmental Agencies;
Inter-Authority Agencies;

Joint Operations by Public Authorities;
Voluntary Organizations.

7   Miscellaneous Expenses

Subscriptions;
Grants to Voluntary Associations;
Other Expenses.

8   Debt Charges

Cash Flow Management;
Non-borrowing Sources of Finance;

   Government Capital Grants;
   Contribution from Revenue;
   Internal Capital Funding;
   Leaseback, Leasing and Renting;
   Capital Receipts;

Borrowing Techniques;
Overall Considerations.

9   Income

Excludes Central and Local Taxation;
Government Grants;
Sales;

   Publications;
   Produce;
   Catering;
   Miscellaneous Sales;

Fees and charges;
Rents; Housing;
Commercial and Industrial Rents;
Operational Rents;
Miscellaneous Rents;
Interest Receivable;
Other Sources of Income, eg Lotteries, Advertising
Sales.

10 Capital Expenditure

Long-term Nature of Capital Investments;

Capital Plans;

Capital Programmes;

Capital Projects;

   Strict Budgetary Controls;
   Performance and Monitoring.

Better Procedures Can be Undertaken with Existing
Staffing Levels.

Appendix D

Effectiveness Audit Flowchart

The following flowchart depicts the interrelationship of the major programme results review activities (i.e. effectiveness measurement) devised by the United States General Accounting Office.

A: Pre-review familiarization and planning activities

A1.   Selection of program for review.

A2.   Receipt of assignment request or RFP.

A3.   Assignment clarification activities:
 – assignment objective
 – basic review and reporting requirements
 – program objectives
 – potential problems.

A4.   Are the assignment objectives and requirements clearly understood?

A5.   Obtain additional clarification from the review requestor.

A6.   Conduct a preliminary survey to
 – verify program objectives
 – become familiar with program operation
 – identify the existing system for measuring program effectiveness.

A7.   Based on preliminary program knowledge and review agency capabilities, should program results review be pursued?

A8.   Terminate further involvement; if necessary, prepare written justification.

A9.   Select an appropriate review strategy.

A10. Prepare work plan and/or bid proposal outlining proposed strategy, timetables, and resource requirements.

A11. Is work plan (bid proposal) acceptable?

A12. Can work plan (bid proposal) be modified to be made acceptable?

A13. Terminate further involvement.

A14. Modify work plan (bid proposal) as necessary.

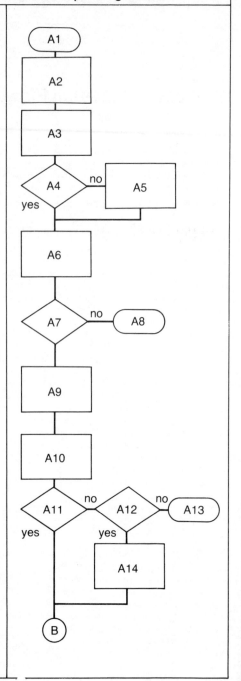

B: Assessing management's effectiveness measurement system

B1. Identify and document management's system for measuring program effectiveness.

B2. Identify program objectives not subject to effectiveness measurement; consider feasibility of an ad hoc system for these objectives.

B3. Assess the validity and suffiency of the performance indicators.

B4. Are the performance indicators valid and sufficient?

B5. Does management agree with the identified deficiency?

B6. Without the approval or authority to independently develop an ad hoc measurement system, terminate further work relative to the deficient condition and prepare an appropriate justification statement.

B7. Modify or monitor the modification of management's effectiveness measurement system.

B8. Assess the accuracy of the performance indicator data.

B9. Do the data sources and collection techniques provide reliable and unbiased data?

B10. Does management agree with the identified deficiency?

B11. Same as 'B6' above.

B12. Same as 'B7' above.

B13. Assess the appropriateness of the performance standards.

B14. Are the performance standards appropriate?

B15. Does management agree with the identified deficiency?

B16. Same as 'B6' above.

B17. Same as 'B7' above.

B18. Based on either the existing or modified effectiveness measurement system, is the program achieving the desired level of program results?

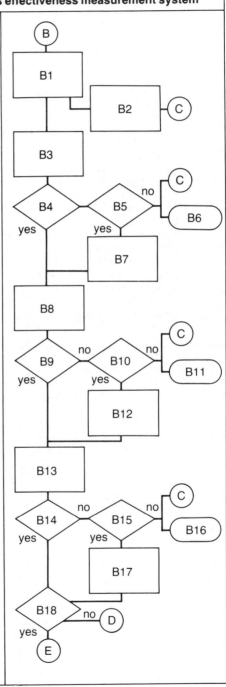

VMA–N

C: Using an *ad hoc* system to measure effectiveness

C1. Conduct a feasibility study.
C2. Can an acceptable ad hoc measurement system be developed?
C3. Document reason(s) an ad hoc system cannot be used to determine program effectiveness.
C4. Terminate further efforts to measure that program objective.
C5. Design the ad hoc system.
C6. Is the ad hoc system acceptable to program management?
C7. Identify the cause of disagreement.
C8. Based on the previously established conflict resolution agreeements, can the review agency proceed to use the ad hoc system?
C9. Terminate further work relative to the use of an ad hoc system.
C10. Revise the ad hoc measurement system, if required.
C.11 Collect the necessary performance indicator data.
C.12 Determine the level of program effectiveness.
C.13 Is the program achieving its intended results?

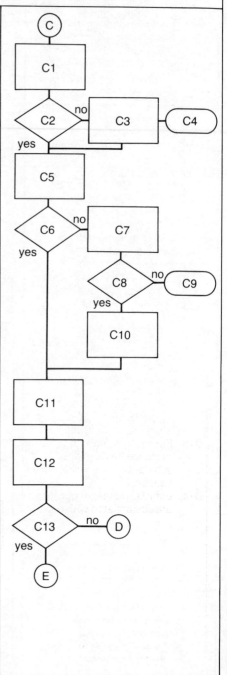

D: Identifying causes that inhibit program effectiveness

D1. For each objective not being satisfactorily achieved, identify possible causes or constraints that may inhibit increased effectiveness.

D2. Interview program personnnel.

D3. Review previously collected performance data.

D4. Review previous audit reports or evaluation studies.

D5. Review program plans, policies, procedures and controls.

D6. Observe program operations.

D7. Interview program clients or beneficiaries.

D8. Assess the sufficiency of program resources.

D9. Analyse program trends.

D10. Examine the program's external environment.

D11. Interview other individuals knowledgeable of the program or its environment.

D12. Substantiate the validity of the identified causes:
  – agreeable to program management.
  – increasing the scope.
  – corroboration.
  – regression analysis.

D13. For each cause, can sufficient evidence be developed to substantiate the validity of the cause?

D14. Either eliminate or qualify unsubstantiated causes.

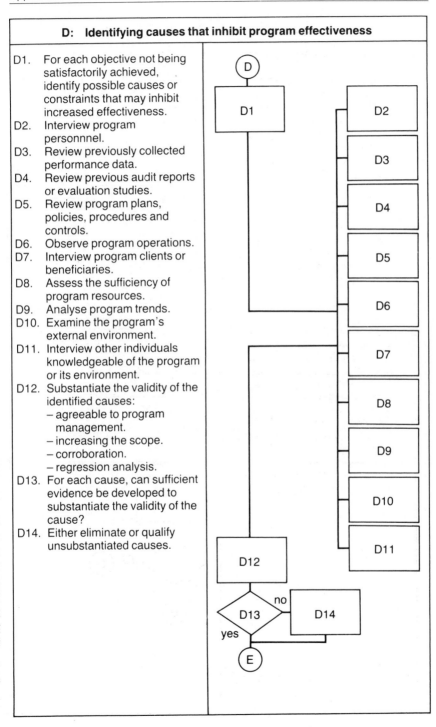

E: Obtaining supplemental information

E1.   Solicit program cost data.
E2.   Can program cost data be obtained or developed?
E3.   Document the reason this data cannot be obtained or developed?
E4.   Develop or estimate the cost of eliminating or reducing the influence of the validated causes of ineffectiveness.
E5.   Would significant costs be incurred to improve program effectiveness?
E6.   Estimate the benefits that would be derived from these costly proposals.
E7.   Has management considered alternative operating strategies that might yield the desired results at a lower cost?
E8.   Document the status of these alternatives.
E9.   During the review, were potential unintended results (i.e. side-effects) observed or identified that might be attributable to the program?
E10. Determine the significance of these unintended results.

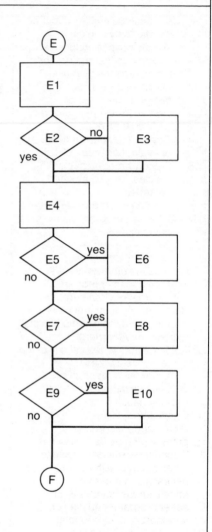

F: Communicating the review findings

F1.   Was the review able to establish a definitive determination of program effectiveness?

F2.   Document and report the reason(s) that hindered the determination of program effectiveness.

F3.   Report the level of effectiveness and the means (i.e. effectiveness measurement system) used to determine it.

F4.   If management's effectiveness measurement system was used to determine effectiveness, did it operate adequately?

F5.   Document and report the nature of the inadequacy.

F6.   Propose recommendations to correct the deficient condition.

F7.   Report the verified adequacy of management't effectiveness measurement system.

F8.   Was the program found to be achieving its desired results?

F9.   Document and report the causes that inhibit increased effectiveness.

F10. Can cost-effective recommendations be proposed?

F11. Report the excessive costs or other disbenefits that would be necessary to improve effectiveness; recommend either program reduction or termination, if appropriate.

F12. Formulate and propose recommendations or alternatives to improve future program effectiveness.

F13. Issue report to appropriate government decision-makers.

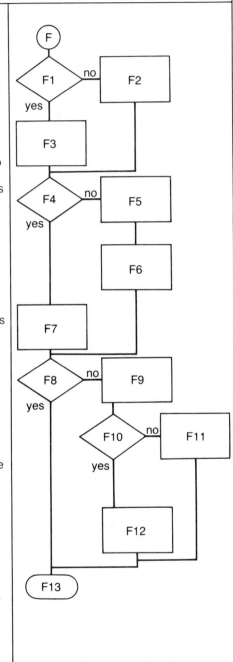

Bibliography

Abel-Smith, B., 'Value for Money in Health Services', Bulletin, July 1974, pp. 17-28.

Adams, J.W. (Chairman), Report of the Special Committee to Examine the Role of the Auditor, Canadian Institute of Chartered Accountants, 1978. (Complete report published in C.A. Magazine, April 1978.)

Allard, J.C., 'Comprehensive Auditing In Crown Corporations - A Stronger Handle on the Public Purse', C.A. Magazine, February 1981.

American Accounting Association, Report of the Committee on Concepts of Accounting Applicable to the Public Sector, 1970-71, Sarasota, Florida.

American Institute of Certified Public Accountants, Hospital Audit Guide (1972), Audits of Colleges and Universities (1973), Audits of Voluntary Health and Welfare Organizations (1974), Audits of State and Local Governmental Units (1974), Accounting Principles and Reporting Practices for Certain Non-profit Organizations (1978).

Anthony, R.N., 'Can Non-profit Organizations Be Well Managed?' Vital Speeches of the Day, 18 February 1971.

Anthony, R.N., Financial Accounting in Non-business Organizations, Financial Accounting Standards Board, Stanford, Conn., 1978.

Anthony, R.N. and Harzlinger, H., Management Control in Non-profit Organizations, Homewood, Irwin 1975.

Association of Government Accountants (USA), Operational Auditing, Monograph Number One, 1978.

Australia, Public Accounts and Expenditure Committee, Parliament of Victoria, Review of the Audit Act 1958 (A Discussion Paper), Melbourne, 1981.

Australia, Joint Committee of Public Accounts, The Form and Standard of Financial Statements for Commonwealth Undertakings - A Discussion Paper, (Report No. 199), Canberra, 1982.

Australia, Report of the Auditor General upon Audits, Examinations and Inspections under the Audit and other Acts, Australian Government Publishing Service, Canberra, 1983.

Australia, Public Service Board, Interdepartmental Advisory Committee on Internal Audit, Paper No. 61, A Survey of Internal Audit in the Australian Public Service, Australian Government Publishing Service, Canberra, 1983.

Basildon Council, A Classification of English Non-Metropolitan District Councils, to assist in the selection of comparators, June 1981.

Berggren, G.R., 'Effectiveness Auditing in Sweden's Central Government Administration', unpublished paper available from The Swedish National Audit Bureau.

Bird, P., and Morgan-Jones, P., Financial Reporting by Charities, ICAEW, 1981.

Briston, R., and Perks, R., 'The External Auditor - His Role and Cost to Society', Accountancy, Vol 88, No 11, pp.48-52.

Canada, Corporate Planning and Development Division, City of Thunder Bay, Performance Measurement Manual and Catalogue, December 1980.

Canada, Program Evaluation: An Introduction, Office of the Auditor General of Canada, Ottawa, February 1981.

Canada, An Approach to Comprehensive Auditing, Office of the Auditor General , Ottawa, September 1981.

Canada, Audit Guide: Auditing of Procedures for Effectiveness, Office of Auditor General of Canada, Ottawa, 1981.

Canada, Audit Guide: Auditing of Efficiency, Office of the Auditor General , Ottawa, January 1981.

Canada, Guide on the Program Evaluation Function, Office of
the Comptroller General, Ottawa, May 1981.

Canada, Royal Commission on Financial Management and
Accountability: Final Report, Government Publishing Centre,
Ottawa, 1979.

Canadian Comprehensive Auditing Foundation, Comprehensive
Auditing - An Overview (1980); Comprehensive Auditing - A
New Approach to Public Sector Accountability in Canada
(1980); The Role of Auditing in Canadian Municipal
Administration (1983), Ottawa.

Canadian Institute of Chartered Accountants, Financial
Reporting for Non-profit Organizations, Toronto, 1980.

Cate, G.M., 'Federal Accounting: Procedures in Search of a
Philosophy', The Government Accountants Journal (USA),
Winter 1978-79.

Chambers, A.D., Internal Auditing, Pitman, 1981.

Chapman, J.T., New Zealand Audit Office Experience With
Effectiveness And Efficiency Audits, a paper delivered at
the University of Melbourne, Department of Accounting,
February 1983.

Clarke, R., Public Expenditure, Management and Control,
MacMillan Press, London, 1978.

CIPFA, Statements on Internal Audit Practice - Public Sector,
London, 1979.

CIPFA, Standards of the External Audit of Local Authorities
and other Public Bodies Subject to Audit under Part III of
the Local Government Finance Act 1982, London, 1982.

Colville, I. and Tomkins, C., 'Value for Money in the Public
Sector: (2) Economy, Effectiveness and the Role of the
Auditor', Local Finance, pp.13-22, 1981.

Connolly, D.M., 'Internal Audit - The Poor Relation of the
Public Service', Australian Journal of Public Administration,
Vol XXXIX, No 1, March 1980.

Cooke, T.C. and Glynn J.J., 'Fixed Asset Replacement in a
Recession', Accountancy, November 1981, Vol 92, No 1054,
pp.83-85.

Department of the Environment, Publication of Financial and
other Information by Local Authorities: A Consultation
document, London, 1980.

De Paula, F.C. and Attwood, F.A., Auditing Principles and
Practice, Pitman, 1983.

Du Cann, E., The Parliamentarian, June 1977.

Epping Forest District Council, Report of a Study of Five
District Councils, August 1976.

Fielden, J. and Robertson, D.,'Value for money and
performance review in local government', Management
Accounting, October 1980, pp.26-30.

Financial Accounting Standards Board, Conceptual Framework
for Financial Accounting and Reporting: Objectives of
Financial Reporting by Non-business Organizations, Stamford,
Connecticut, 1978.

Glynn, J.J., 'The Value for Money Trend', Accountancy,
December 1982, pp.129-130.

Glynn, J.J., 'Effectiveness Auditing - Its Role in the
Public Sector', Accountancy, March 1983, pp.135-136.

Granhof, M.H. and Boerman, A.L., 'Local Government Audit:
Obstacles and Opportunities'; in State Audit - Developments
in Public Accountability, edited by Geist, B., MacMillan,
1981, pp.349-362.

Gross, M.J., (Jr), 'New audit guides - their significance
for nonprofit organizations', Journal of Accounting, April
1974, pp. 76-82.

Hatch, J. and Redwood, J., Value for Money Audits, Centre
for Policy Studies, London, 1981.

Hatry, H.P., Claren, S.N., Von Houten, T., Woodward, J.P.
and Don Vito, P.A., Efficiency Measurement for Local
Government Services, The Urban Institute, Washington D.C.,
1979.

Heald, D., Public Expenditure, Martin Robertson and Company
Ltd, 1983.

Heclo, H. and Wildavsky, A., The Government of Public Money,
MacMillan Press, London, 1974.

Heeny, A., The Things that are Caesar's, Toronto, 1972.

Henke, E.O., Audit Reports for Not-For-Profit Organisations, The Texas CPA, April 1972, pp. 20-24.

Henke, E.O., Introduction to Non-profit Organization Accounting, Wadsworth Inc., 1980.

Henley, D. Sir, 'External Audit', Chapter 7 of Public Sector Accounting and Financial Control jointly authored with Holtham, C., Likierman, A. and Perrin, J., Van Nostrand Reinhold (UK) Co Ltd., 1983.

Hepworth, N.P., The Finance of Local Government, 6th edition, George Allen and Unwin, 1980.

Hill, D.J., 'Innovations in Government Accounting', in Government Accounting and Budgeting, edited by Hardman, D.J., Prentice-Hall Australia, 1982.

Holtham, C. and Stewart, J., Value for Money A Framework for Action, Institute of Local Government Studies, University of Birmingham, 1981

Hopwood, A., Edgeley, R. and Anderson, E.,'Social Accounting' (three separate articles), Public Finance and Accountancy, September 1980, pp. 12-17.

Ivarrson, S.I., 'Effectiveness Control in a Program Budgeting System', The Swedish National Audit Bureau, 1974.

LAMSAC, Value for Money - Studies in Local government, London 1980.

Lapsley, I. and Owen A.J., Public-sector Capital Assets Accounting and Finance, Warwick, CIEBR, 1978.

Lapsley, I. and Prowle, M.J., Audit in the National Health Service: a Conceptial Perspective, Warwick, CIEBR, 1978.

Lathe, S., The Value for Money Audit in not-for-profit organizations, Cost and Management (Canada), November - December, 1978, pp. 51-54.

Layfield, F. Sir (Chairman), Local Government Finance, Report of the Committee of Enquiry, HMSO London, Cmnd. 6453, 1976.

Macdonell, J.J., 'Comprehensive Auditing - A New Approach to Public Sector Accountability in Canada', a paper presented to The Second Seminar of Senior Government Audit Institutions, Mexico City, 1980.

Maynard, B.A. (Chairman), Advisory Committee on Local Government Audit - First Report, London, HMSO, 1980.

Milburn, J.A., Audit reports for non-profit organizations, Canadian Chartered Accountant, December 1969, pp. 429-433.

Morse, E.H., 'Performance and Operational Auditing', The Journal of Accountancy, June 1971, pp.41-46.

National Council on Government Accounting (USA), Government Accounting and Financial and Reporting Principles, Chicago, Illinois, March 1979.

New Zealand, Office of The Controller And Auditor General, Report on the Effectiveness And Efficiency of the Canterbury United Council, Wellington, 1983.

Owen, A.J., Health Authority Capital Budgeting: the State of the Art in Theory and Practice, Warwick, CIEBR, 1978.

Pendelbury, M.,and Jones, R., Municipal Disclosure In England - Another Market for Excuses? Research Studies in Business and Finance, UWIST, 1980.

Perrin, J., Research Issues in the Public And Not-For-Profit Sectors, Warwick, CIEBR, 1980.

Pratt, M.J., Auditing, Longman, 1983.

Redwood, J. and Hatch, J., Controlling Public Industries, Basil Blackwell, Oxford, 1982.

Royal Commission on the National Health Service, Report, Cmnd. 7615, London HMSO, 1979.

Rutman, L., Planning Useful Evaluations, Saga Library of Social Research, Vol 96, Saga Publications Ltd, 1980.

Scantlebury, D.L. and Raaum, R.B., Operational Auditing, Association of Government Accountants, Washington D.C., 1978.

Seidler, L.J. and Seidler, L.L., Social Accounting : Theory, Issues and Cases, Melville Publishing, California, 1975.

Sherer, M. and Kent, D., Auditing and Accountability, Pitman, 1983.

Smith, B., 'Control in British Government: A Problem of Accountability', Policy Studies Journal, Vol 9, 1980, pp.1163-74.

Sweden, Budgeting In The Swedish Government, National Audit Bureau, Stockholm, 1978.

Sweden, Efficiency And Effectiveness Control of Public Enterprises - The audit problem, National Audit Bureau, Stockholm, 1978.

Sweden, Effectiveness Auditing in Sweden's Central Government Administration, National Audit Bureau, Stockholm, 1980.

Sweden, Performance Analysis - Why and How?, National Audit Bureau, Stockholm, 1980.

Sweden, Auditing of Social-Welfare Sysytems, National Audit Bureau, Stockholm, 1983.

Tanner, B., Likierman, A., Magee, C. and Osmolski, R. and Holtham, C., 'Measuring Peformance'(four articles), Public Finance and Accountancy, March 1980, pp. 12-21.

The Role of the Comptroller and Auditor General, Cmnd.7845, HMSO London, 1980.

Treasury, Economic Progress Reports, especially Nos. 139,145 and 163, HMSO London, 1981-1983.

USA, General Accounting Office, Using Auditing To Improve Efficiency & Economy: A case study of an efficiency and economy audit of a local government activity, Washington DC, 1975.

USA, General Accounting Office, Guidelines For Economy and Efficiency Audits of Federally Assisted Programs. (Exposure Draft), Washington DC, 1978.

USA, General Accounting Office, Comprehensive Approaches For Planning And Conducting A Program Results Review, Washington DC, 1978.

USA, General Accounting Office, Using Broad Scope Auditing to Serve Management, Audit Supplement Series No. 10, Washington DC, 1978.

USA, General Accounting Office, Standards for Audit of Government, Organizations, Programs, Activities and Functions, (The Yellow Book), Washington D.C., 1972.

USA, General Accounting Office, Exposure Draft: Comprehensive Approach for Planning and Conducting a Program Results Review, Washington D.C., 1978.

Vatter, W.J., 'State of the Art - Non-business Accounting', The Accounting Review, Vol. LIV, No. 3, July 1979, pp. 574-584.

Webb, K. and Hatry, H.P., Obtaining Citizen Feedback: The Application of Citizen Survey to Local Government, The Urban Institute, Washington D.C., 1973.

Index